MW01602250

Other Kaplan Books for High School Students

Essential Review: High School Biology

Essential Review: High School Chemistry

Essential Review: High School Mathematics I

Essential Review: High School Mathematics II

Essential Review: High School Mathematics III

High School 411

Yale Daily News Guide to Summer Programs

No-Stress Guide to the Exit-Level TAAS*

*Texas Assessment of Academic Skills

Cynthia and Drew Johnson

Simon & Schuster

SYDNEY · LONDON · SINGAPORE · NEW YORK

Kaplan Books
Published by Simon & Schuster
1230 Avenue of the Americas
New York, NY 10020

For bulk sales to schools, colleges, and universities, please contact: Vice President of
Special Sales, Simon & Schuster Special Markets, 1230 Avenue of the Americas,
8th Floor, New York, NY 10020.

Project Editor: Ruth Baygell

Contributing Editors: Marti Garlett and Steve Johnson

Cover Design: Cheung Tai

Interior Page Design and Layout: Jobim Rose

Production Editor: Maude Spekes

Managing Editor: Dave Chipps

Executive Editor: Del Franz

Manufactured in the United States of America

January 2000

10 9 8 7 6 5 4 3 2 1

Library of Congress Cataloging-in-Publication Data is available.

ISBN: 0-684-87091-6

All of the practice questions in this book were created by the author to illustrate
question types. They are not actual test questions. For more useful information on the
TAAS, visit the Texas Education Agency's Division of Student Assessment Web site at
www.tea.state.tx.us/student.assessment/.

Contents

Authors

Cynthia Johnson is the author of several educational books for young people, including *Word Smart Junior* and *Writing Smart Junior*, both of which received the prestigious Parent's Choice Gold Award in 1995, and were included in *Curriculum Administrator* magazine's list of "Top 100" educational products for 1996.

Drew Johnson is the author of *Kidding Around Austin!*, a travel activity book for children, and coauthor of *Kaplan Learning Power*, a guide to improving study skills. Drew is currently an education writer and editor creating workbook, textbook, and worldwide Web-based educational materials for students of all ages.

Welcome to the TAAS

The following manuscript has been translated into English from its original language, Kronhorsti, an alien language spoken by the inhabitants of the fourth planet orbiting the sun Cygnus X-7.
—X!Frumious

TO: The Most Supreme Ruler of the Planet Kronhorst

FROM: X!Frumious the Explorer, currently stationed on Earth

RE: The discovery of standardized tests within the universe

Dear Most Grand Leader of Kronhorst,

Greetings from Earth! As you know, my team of explorers and I have been spending some time on this planet to learn more about its culture and people. For the most part, I can tell you that human beings are intelligent, kind, and helpful, unless you happen to be driving too slow in the left lane of the highway; then, it's a WHOLE different story, and not one I can tell you with the interplanetary censors around. It is interesting to note that like every other species we have encountered in the universe, humans have invented the sport which we know as **clickvellsgerstoof** and which they call "professional wrestling." There is, however, one thing that humans have invented that exists nowhere else in known space—standardized testing.

Eager to learn all we could about standardized tests, my crew and I headed our spaceship to our usual landing spot. Unfortunately, we could not find a parking space in Roswell, New Mexico, so we went east a bit and landed in Texas. Lucky for us we did, because once in Texas we discovered the **Texas Assessment of Academic Skills**, also known as the **TAAS**. This standardized test is given to all Texas students in grades 3 through 10.

Although the TAAS has been around for most of the 1990s, recent legislation was passed making the test more important than ever. The TAAS is now being used to grade how well schools and school districts are performing. However, in 2003, all third graders taking the 3ʳᵈ Grade Test must get a passing score in order to be promoted to the fourth grade. In 2004, this same group must pass the 4th Grade TAAS to get into the fifth grade, and so on. By 2010, the TAAS will be mandatory for promotion for all grades, unless new legislation is introduced to change this format.

Currently, the 10th Grade TAAS, or Exit-Level TAAS, has the most impact on Texas students, since they are required to pass this test in order to graduate from high school. It is the only TAAS that everyone currently has to pass, although some school districts have made passing the other TAAS tests a requirement for promotion as well. The Exit-Level TAAS is summarized in the chart below:

Overview Exit-Level TAAS

Number of sections	3 (Reading, Mathematics, and Writing)
Number of questions	48 reading questions 60 math questions 40 writing questions plus an essay
Correct answers needed to pass	roughly 70% for all sections;
Reading:	33 out of 48
Math:	40 out of 60
Writing:	Answer varies depending on how well a student fares on the essay (the better the essay, the fewer of the 40 questions needed to pass)
Format	Except for writing essay, all questions are multiple-choice with 4–5 answer choices
Time given for test	untimed

Students have to pass all three sections in order to graduate high school and must retake any one section that they fail. Retests are given in the fall, spring, and summer. While it's good to be given extra chances to succeed, taking the same kind of standardized test over and over again is not a fun experience. As you can see, O Great Ruler, the Exit TAAS is much harder than our Kronhorstian tests, and Earthlings have only one brain, which strangely enough is located in their heads. No wonder so many Texans were talking about this test.

In the spirit of pioneering, I, X!Frumious the Explorer, decided to become the first Kronhorstian to take and pass the Exit-Level TAAS. I put on the regulation human disguise—these Earthlings have only two legs, how can they dance?—and enrolled at Eastbury High School in Houston. I made some mistakes on the first day I was in school, such as eating a cafeteria bench, but soon I fit right in with the rest of the student body.

After attending some classes, I soon realized that having a college degree from a distant planet does not mean you can pass a tenth grade state standardized test. This is because the TAAS was specifically designed by the Texas Education Agency to see how well students were mastering the state's curriculum, known as **Texas Essential Knowledge and Skills** (TEKS). Since the TAAS questions mirror the TEKS objectives, the TAAS provides a way for the Texas Education Agency to determine whether or not a student has mastered the TEKS objectives for his or her grade level.

It's a good arrangement, but it meant I was going to need human help if I wanted to pass the Exit TAAS. Fortunately for me, I found a group of five Eastbury students who asked me if I wanted to join their study group to help prepare for the test. It turns out that the phrase "study group" means the same thing in English as it does in Kronhorsti, except in a human study group there's no major surgery involved. This study group already had people who were specialists in the different test-taking areas, but they needed someone to take notes for the whole group. I eagerly volunteered to be the study group note taker, and everyone was happy.

The members of my study group are:

Daniel Bryant, who specializes in test-taking strategies

Ridley Anderson, an expert at Mathematics

Alexis Wolfe, the Reading Section guru

Jorge Benitez, Foreign Exchange Student. Since he's from another country, Jorge is an expert on how English is supposed to be written, so he's in charge of the Writing section questions

William Walker, also known as "Willy H_2SO_4," who is in charge of the Writing Composition part

And of course there is me, **X!Frumious**, the group recorder.

O Exalted Ruler, I have provided the notes of our study group meetings on the following pages so that you might learn as much about the Exit-Level TAAS as I have. I have also included TAAS-like questions throughout this book so that you might try out your skill on sample problems. It is my belief that anyone who reads these pages, learns the techniques discussed, and practices them on the TAAS will be able to pass all three sections, regardless of what planet they originally came from.

I Remain Your Humble Citizen,

X!Frumious

X!Frumious the Explorer, of the planet Kronhorst

Chapter 1

Test-Taking Strategies

Session Leader: Daniel Bryant

O Most Mighty One, here are the notes from my first study group meeting. Whenever Daniel wrote something down on the blackboard, I have included that drawing among my notes.

–X!Frumious

NAME: Daniel J. Bryant

BORN: March 22, 1984
Rollingwood, Texas

NOTES: Daniel actually likes standardized tests, which puts him in the same category as about one half of one percent of American students. He took the SAT at age 12 for the first time as part of a Duke University study, and has taken the SAT every year since. Daniel hopes to turn a good score on the PSAT test into a National Honor Society Scholarship to college. He owns a dog, a Malamute name Abacab.

Daniel: First, I would like to thank everyone—Ridley, Alexis, Jorge, Willy, and X!Frumious—for showing up to the meeting on time. Before we start, I asked X!Frumious to go to the store and get us some snacks for the group. How did that go, X!Frumy?

X!Frumious: Just fine, Dan. I was walking down the aisle with barbecue and picnic supplies and I found these delightful items. They really taste great, I think.

Daniel: X!Frumious, those are charcoal. You're eating gasoline-soaked briquettes.

Ridley: Let's just skip the snacks for now. Agreed?

Daniel: Good. Now, down to business. In order to succeed on the Exit TAAS, there are eight main test-taking strategies you need to master to get the score you want. The first strategy sounds very simple, but it's crucial: Get to know the format of the test inside and out.

Strategy 1

Understand the format of the test like the back of your hand.

If you know what to expect, you will feel more confident about your ability to do well. Under such high-stakes pressure, it is crucial that you take control and not get bogged down or agonize.

This means you should know exactly how many questions are in each section, which multiple-choice questions have four answer choices and which have five, and most of all, how many questions you need to answer correctly in order to receive a passing score.

Willy: Why is this important? We've all taken some form of the TAAS before.

Daniel: That might be true, but knowing exactly what is ahead of you on the three test-taking days achieves many positive goals. First, knowing the format relieves some of the uncertainty about the test, and familiarizing yourself with the different question types should help you avoid becoming rattled or too nervous to do a good job on the test.

Let's face it; since this TAAS test determines whether or not we get to graduate high school, there's a lot of pressure on us to do well. The normal human reaction when faced with such a high-stakes test is to feel nervous and anxious about the exam. The problem is, feeling nervous or anxious while taking a standardized test almost always leads to a lower score. Granted, I don't expect y'all to be excited about the TAAS, but you do need to eliminate any anxiety in order to improve your score. One way to do this is by familiarizing yourself with the exam, so that instead of dreading this scary, unknown test, you can go in knowing not only what to expect on the TAAS, but what you need to do in order to get a passing score.

Ridley: So Familiarity = Confidence on the TAAS?

Daniel: That's right. But understanding the test format doesn't just help you before the test, it also prevents you from freaking out during the test. We all know people who have suffered from "test meltdown," where they come across a question that they don't understand and so panic. In a situation with less pressure, they might be able to handle it, but with high school graduation hanging in the balance, a weird question can really affect their focus. By knowing what to expect, you won't get unnerved.

Willy: I'll need an example before I agree with your theory.

Daniel: I'll give you two, Willy. First of all, in the math section the first 20 questions have four multiple-choice answers, but then the rest of the questions have five answer choices. It's a minor change, sure, but if you don't know it's coming, it can be unsettling. You ask yourself, "why did they do that?" and while you're trying to figure that out, you're doing nothing to improve your TAAS Math score.

The existence of field questions is another thing everyone should know before starting the Exit TAAS tests. On every section, there are about eight questions that DON'T count toward your score. They're called field test questions because the Texas Education Agency (TEA) is trying out these questions to see if it should include them on future exams. So while this serves a good purpose—it helps guarantee that your TAAS test is similar to the TAAS tests on other years—it also means that roughly one out of every eight questions on the test does nothing to help your score. Some of these questions are really easy and others are really hard. If you try to answer one of the tough field test questions, and spend fifteen minutes working yourself into a lather over it, then you've just worked yourself up over a problem that means nothing.

Alexis: Is there a way to recognize a field test question, and then just skip over it?

Daniel: Unfortunately, no. Just be aware that these questions exist, and don't get frazzled by any one question, because it might not count. And even if that one tough question does count, there's still no need to be worried. Remember, there are only two real grades on each TAAS section: pass or fail. For instance, it doesn't matter if you get 40 or 60 questions right on the math section, since both are passing scores. The person who makes a perfect score on a section gets no special bonus for doing so. What this means is that no single question is

---

Information

*In every section on the TAAS, there are about eight questions that don't count toward your score. They're called **field test questions** because the TEA is trying out these questions for possible use on future exams. This means that roughly one out of every eight questions on the test does not affect your score. There is no way to recognize a field test question, however, so just work through the test normally and don't get worked up if you are having trouble on any one problem. In the end, that problem might not count!*

critical to your overall test score, so if you are having trouble with a particular problem, don't get bent out of shape about it.

Daniel: The next test-taking strategy you all must learn is the concept of pacing.

Work through the TAAS at a consistently steady pace. This means you never rush through a question and make a hurried mistake, and you also don't spend too long on any one problem.

X!Frumious: But the TAAS is untimed. Why not take as much time as you want?

Daniel: Just because you have eight hours to take a test doesn't mean you should take eight hours. Spending thirty minutes on a single question does not help your overall score if you exhaust yourself mentally answering it. Also, since the TAAS is given over three consecutive days, you don't want to burn yourself out on the first day.

The key to surviving these three days of testing is to maintain a steady pace. Spend at least a minute on each question—if you go faster you may make a careless error—but never more than five minutes. The best way to approach every section is to use a Two-Pass System. Go through each test section two times. First, complete the easy problems. Then go back and work through the more difficult ones.

> **Strategy 2**
>
> *Maintain a consistent pace throughout the test. Don't rush through any one question. Even if you think you can answer a question in 10 seconds, remember that the test is designed to challenge you, so seemingly obvious answers may not be what you think. Similarly, don't spend too much time on any one question. If you do, you might become drained and lose the focus you need to solve the remaining problems.*

> **Strategy 3**
>
> *Take short breaks during the test to help you relieve mental fatigue. If you feel yourself getting mentally tired, just put your pencil down and take a minute to stretch. Stretch your arms, stretch your fingers, clear your mind, and then refocus your thoughts back on the test.*

Willy: Daniel, you said I should spend at least a minute on every question, but why should I do that if I can figure out the question in ten seconds?

Strategy 4

Approach every test section using a Two-Pass System:

* First, go through each TAAS section and answer all the questions you feel most comfortable with.

* When you have finished your first pass, go back through and spend more time on the harder questions.

Daniel: The reason, Willy, is because the test has traps designed to trip up students rushing through the TAAS tests. You see, on most tests you take during your educational career, going fast helps you get to more problems in a limited time. But the writers of the TAAS know this, so they've included incorrect answer choices that students might pick if they are in a hurry. Here's an example:

1. A teacher is making 7 different walking sticks for use in the school play. If each stick requires $3\frac{3}{4}$ feet of wood, how much wood is needed altogether for the 7 walking sticks?

   A. $10\frac{3}{4}$

   B. $17\frac{1}{2}$

   C. $21\frac{3}{4}$

   D. $26\frac{1}{4}$

   E. Not Here

If a student merely glances at this question and doesn't take the time to properly work out the math, the number that really sticks out in the question is "$3\frac{3}{4}$."

Looking at the answer choices, both A and C have $\frac{3}{4}$ in them, and C looks especially good because at first glance 7 multiplied by $3\frac{3}{4}$ equals $21\frac{3}{4}$. So a student who was rushing through a section and not keeping a consistent pace would pick C and rapidly move along.

Ridley: However, if that same student took a minute to answer the question, he or she would multiply $3\frac{3}{4}$ by 7 and get $26\frac{1}{4}$, or answer choice D. This doesn't appear a likely answer, but if you take the time and do the math, it is the correct answer.

Daniel: This question illustrates how you can harm your score by going too slow or too fast. Now y'all have an idea of how the two-pass system works. Let's say that you've gone through the first pass, and now you're working on a tougher problem. You spend about five minutes looking over it, but you still don't know how to answer it. Do you leave it blank and then move on? The answer is, NO, NO, NO!!

> **Strategy 5**
>
> *Answer every question—even if you have to guess. Your score is based solely on the number of questions that you answer correctly. You are not penalized for wrong answers, so be sure to answer every question. Any question you skip is a missed opportunity to earn free points.*

Even if you have only a one in five chance of getting the problem right, you should bubble in an oval before you move on to the next question. There's no penalty for answering a question incorrectly on the TAAS, so any question you skip is a missed opportunity for free points.

Willy: Sounds fine, Dan, but if we have only a one in four or five chance on a question, we won't get many questions right.

Daniel: That's true, but the next strategy will help you improve those odds. The technique is called *Process of Elimination*, or *POE*, and it's an effective way of eliminating incorrect answer choices on multiple-choice questions.

Remember everyone, the answer to every TAAS question is right in front of you. You don't have to know it directly off the top of your head, you just have to be able to pick the correct answer out from a list of possible

> **Strategy 6**
>
> *Use the **Process of Elimination** (**POE**) to eliminate wrong answer choices. Every wrong answer choice that you rule out brings you closer to finding the right one.*

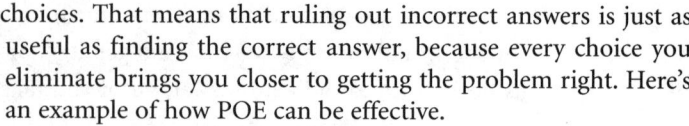

O Mighty Leader, remember your plans to shrink the Alamo to the size of a peanut? Please cancel those plans; something just came up.

choices. That means that ruling out incorrect answers is just as useful as finding the correct answer, because every choice you eliminate brings you closer to getting the problem right. Here's an example of how POE can be effective.

Daniel holds up his right hand clenched in a fist.

2. What am I holding in my hand?

    A. a live rhinoceros
    B. a penny
    C. The Alamo
    D. an eraser

Using Process of Elimination, which answer choices can you eliminate?

Alexis: I eliminated A and C, because your hand is not big enough to hold either of those two items.

Daniel: Most observant, Alexis. So the answer is B or D, and there's no real way to know which is correct, but having a fifty/fifty chance on a series of TAAS questions means you're bound to get some of them right just by guessing.

Now, Alexis, can you explain why you eliminated choices A and C?

Alexis: Well, I thought about what could fit in your hand, and then used common sense to see that it had to be something much smaller than those two choices.

Daniel: Alexis, you used the technique well. When you come to a question, use common sense to think about what the possible answer could be. It sounds simple, and it is, but when placed under high-stakes conditions, many students forget certain basics.

Look for traps that might appear in the question. On the math section there's often one or two incorrect answer choices that contain numbers from the original question, or use numbers from the question in a simplified way. These answer choices are almost always traps, like in the example on the following page.

3. Kerry and her mother used 45 feet of rope from a 60-yard bundle of rope. How many **feet** of rope were left in the bundle?

A. 15 feet
B. 60 feet
C. 105 feet
D. 135 feet

Strategy 7

Use common sense to think about how to answer a question. It sounds simple, and it is, but when placed under high-stakes conditions, many students forget certain basics. Look for traps that might appear in the question.

Before doing the math for this problem, you can eliminate some answers. Choice B just repeats one of the numbers from the problem above, and it can be eliminated as a trap for unsuspecting students. If you rush on this problem, you might pick A or C, since these answers just add or subtract the two numbers in the question. However, if you think about the question, you can see that Kerry and her mother have taken 45 *feet* from a 60 *yard* bundle. That means there's going to be quite a bit of rope left in the bundle, and so choice A is definitely not correct. At this point you can guess between C or D if you can't figure out how to do the math, and considering that C is probably a trap, D would be your best bet. And it's the right answer.

Alexis: But what about the math?

Ridley: Oh, that's simple, you just take 60 yards and multiply by three, so that . . .

Daniel: Ridley could explain the math correctly, Alexis, but she doesn't have to, because we already have the correct answer, D. This is the central advantage of a multiple-choice format; it doesn't matter how you get the right answer, so long as you bubble in the correct oval for the computer to read. In other words, if Ridley does the math properly and answers D, or if you use Process of Elimination to get rid of two choices and then pick D, you both get the same amount of credit.

Jorge: This is good for the math part of the TAAS, but does POE work as well on the other sections?

Daniel: Yes, Process of Elimination works just as well on both the multiple-choice Writing and Reading sections. (But not on the Writing

Composition, as the essay format is immune to POE.) For instance, on the Reading section many incorrect answer choices are words taken directly from the reading passage. These words have nothing to do with the question being asked, but since you might remember reading those words in the passage, the answer choices seem to be correct, or at least reasonable. Consider the following question.

4. Which is a FACT in the passage?

A. The teachers mentioned in the program are distinguished.
B. The postal service is very slow.
C. The skills test will not affect admission into the school.
D. The school library is open 24 hours a day.

Using common sense, which of the above answer choices can you eliminate?

Ridley: I would get rid of D first, since I've never heard of a school library that is open 24 hours a day.

Daniel: So true, Ridley. You can bet, however, that the "school library" is mentioned at least once in the passage, so someone might not cross out D because he or she remembers reading those words in the passage.

Jorge: Choice B does not seem like a good choice, either. It is such a broad statement that it would be hard to prove as a fact, which is what the question is asking. I would eliminate it as well.

Daniel: Good work, Jorge. That leaves just A and C, and since A is a general statement that could be hard to prove as a fact, I would pick C. As it happens, C is the correct answer. Using only POE, we were able to get the correct answer, and we never laid eyes on the reading passage itself.

Daniel: Now, the final strategy: Write all of your work down. If you attempt to solve a problem in your head, you are more likely to make a mistake. By writing it down, you can always retrace your steps.

Once again, this sounds like a simple point, but you would be surprised how many students don't do it. These students just attempt to work the problems in their head, instead of writing their calculations down.

By doing this, these people set themselves up to make mental mistakes. Just the simple mistake of forgetting to carry over a number, or multiply correctly, could lead to the wrong answer. Maybe mental mistakes don't happen that often, but if you write everything down, they'll never happen. Don't risk losing points this way.

Ridley: But what if the answer is just staring right at me?

Daniel: If that's the case, I would ask whether or not it is the correct answer, or whether it's just an attractive *wrong* answer. Think back to the "Bundle of Rope" question we discussed earlier. Answer choices A and C both looked like great choices, if you were in a hurry and didn't do any math on the question. Instead, when you took the time to write out the math, you found out that both of those choices were incorrect.

Jorge: Writing everything down is a very good idea.

Daniel: Yes it is, and all these test-taking strategies are pretty neat, too. If y'all spend the time to get comfortable with them so that you use them on the test, your TAAS scores will improve. If you only think about them today, and then go on to take the test, you probably won't use these techniques and your score will suffer.

One more thing. While these strategies help you mentally prepare for the TAAS, there are some physical preparations you should make before the day of the test as well.

Strategy 8

Write all of your work down.

- On the reading section, summarize the paragraphs you have just read. That way, if a question asks you about information in the passage, you'll have notes to tell you where to look for the answer.

- On the writing section, cross out incorrect answer choices, like double negatives, before you even look at the answer choices. Place a little (–) sign next to these answer choices, so you won't make the mistake of picking them when you analyze the problem.

- On the math section, write out every step you take when solving a problem. If you find that you get stuck, you can go back and retrace your work.

What to Do Right Before the Test

*   The night before the test, make sure you get enough sleep. This doesn't mean you should go to bed earlier than usual, however. If you do that, you'll probably just lie in bed thinking about the test. Instead, try to keep your schedule that night as relaxed and casual as possible.

*   Don't cram for the test. Do a light review and then do something to take your mind off the test. You are better off getting into the proper frame of mind than you are studying one particular technique or another. Do your studying ahead of time, and not on the last night.

*   On the day of the test, make sure you have a good breakfast, but not so filling that you find yourself dying for a nap.

*   On the day of the test, don't take any over-the-counter medication if you don't have to. Having allergies is annoying, but taking medication that muddles your thinking spells trouble for your TAAS score.

Daniel: So, those are the basic strategies for approaching the test. Chances are, you won't come across many problem types that are completely unfamiliar. But if you do, don't panic. If you can figure out what the question is really asking, you can almost always answer it. Put it into your own words so that you simplify what you are looking for, and go from there.

Overview: Test-Taking Strategies

Strategy 1:   *Understand the format of the test like the back of your hand. Knowing what to expect will help boost your confidence to do well.*

Strategy 2:   *Maintain a consistent pace throughout the test. Even if you think you can answer a question in 10 seconds, remember that the test is designed to challenge you. Similarly, don't spend so much time on a question that you get drained or lose focus. So don't rush through—or linger over—any one question.*

Strategy 3:   *Take short breaks during the test to help you relieve mental fatigue. The test is untimed, so make sure you take breaks as necessary. It will help you in the long run.*

Strategy 4:   *Approach every test section using a Two-Pass System. First answer all the questions you are comfortable with, and then go back and work on the harder questions. Just make sure you fill in the correct bubbles on the answer sheet.*

Strategy 5:   *Answer every question on the TAAS, even if you need to guess. There is no penalty for wrong answer choices, so any question you skip is a missed opportunity for free points.*

Strategy 6:   *Use the **Process of Elimination (POE)** to eliminate wrong answer choices. Every wrong answer choice that you rule out brings you closer to finding the right one.*

Strategy 7:   *Use common sense to think about how to answer a question. Often times this will help you rule out certain answer choices.*

Strategy 8:   *Write all of your work down so you can refer easily to it and retrace your steps as needed.*

Mathematics
TAAS

Session Leader: Ridley Anderson

O Munificent Big Guy, what follows are my notes from our second study group meeting, held at the most magnificent place I have ever been in. The place was called a "rec room," and this incredible establishment was located in the basement of Ridley's house, probably for security reasons. I will tell you more about this place, O Scaly One, when we meet in person.
—X!Frumious

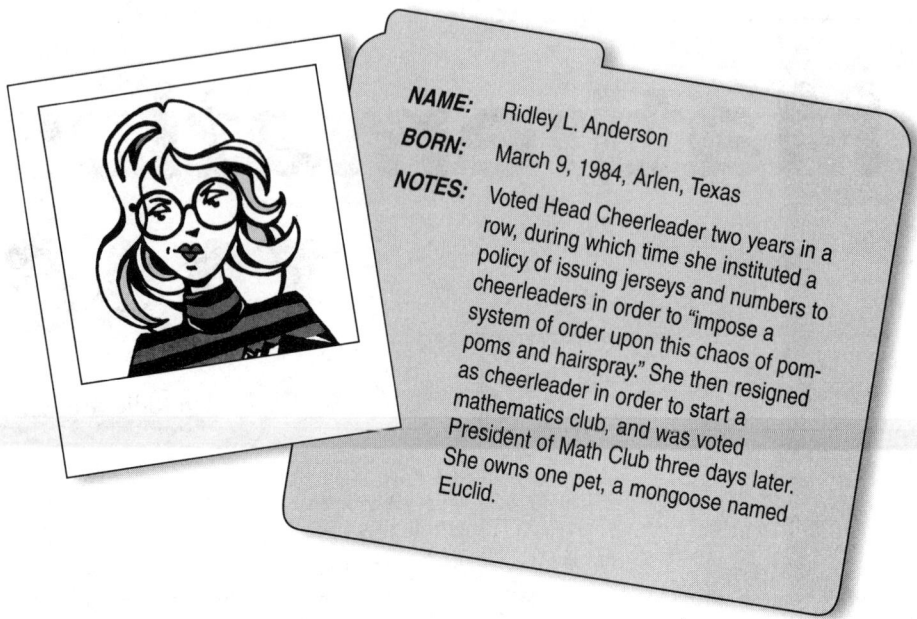

NAME: Ridley L. Anderson

BORN: March 9, 1984, Arlen, Texas

NOTES: Voted Head Cheerleader two years in a row, during which time she instituted a policy of issuing jerseys and numbers to cheerleaders in order to "impose a system of order upon this chaos of pom-poms and hairspray." She then resigned as cheerleader in order to start a mathematics club, and was voted President of Math Club three days later. She owns one pet, a mongoose named Euclid.

Ridley: Hello, I'd like to thank everyone for arriving here on time today. I know that some people find it hard to follow simple directions like "Meet at my house at sixteen seconds past 4:08 p.m."

Daniel: Yes, well, I'd like to take the credit for our punctuality, but we did just follow you home from school. Remember, you said, "Just follow my Mom's car?"

Ridley: Still, it's the thought that counts. Now, my discussion of the Math Section will take 34 minutes, 8 seconds. I would appreciate it, X!Frumious, if you would use a digital stopwatch and notify me at 4 minute, 16 second intervals. Here's a digital watch for you to use. No, X!Frumious, don't eat it.

As Daniel stated earlier, the Math TAAS has 60 multiple-choice questions, as well as 8 field test questions that do not count toward your score. Of the 60 questions, you need to answer at least 40 questions correctly in order to pass this test.

Now, 40 out of 60 translates to two-thirds, one of my favorite fractions. What this means to you is that if you can get 2 out of 3 questions right, you pass the test. While this doesn't mean you should be lazy and answer only 2 out of every 3 questions, it does mean that no single question will determine your grade.

Overview Math TAAS

Number of questions	60 questions plus 8 field-test questions
Correct answers needed to pass	40 out of 60 questions
Format	Multiple-choice questions with 4 or 5 answer choices
Scoring	Your score is based on the number of questions that you answer correctly. You are not penalized for incorrect answers.
Time given for test	Untimed

- Calculators are not permitted.

- Formulas and Measurement Conversions are provided.

Daniel: Ridley's right. There's no need to freak out if you come to a question that you don't understand. It's only one question, and if you do well on the rest of the test, that question won't matter.

Ridley: Also, if it is a hard question for you, it's probably tough for a lot of people. Around 300,000 students take some or all of the Exit-Level TAAS tests each year, so you are not alone in your worries about any one problem.

Willy: Speaking of questions, what kinds of questions are on the Math TAAS?

Ridley: To be precise, there are 13 kinds of questions on the Math TAAS.

Information

The Math TAAS is designed by the Texas Education Agency (TEA) to see how well students have mastered the state's math curriculum, known as **Texas Essential Knowledge and Skills (TEKS)**. There are 13 TAAS objectives designed to match this curriculum.

Overview TAAS Math Objectives

TAAS Objective	No. of Questions on Math TAAS
1. Number Concepts	4
2. Algebraic/Math Relationships and Functions	4
3. Geometric Properties and Relationships	4
4. Measurement Concepts	4
5. Probability and Statistics	4
6. Use of Addition to Solve Problems	4
7. Use of Subtraction to Solve Problems	4
8. Use of Multiplication to Solve Problems	4
9. Use of Division to Solve Problems	4
10. Problem Solving Using Estimation	4
11. Problem Solving Using Solution Strategies	8
12. Problem Solving Using Mathematical Representation	8
13. Evaluation of the Reasonableness of a Solution	4

Ridley: This seems like a lot to learn, but many of these objectives overlap, so it's not as bad as you might think. Also, the TEA has done us a favor and tests only certain objectives on certain problems. I call this . . . "A Tale of Three Tests."

The inclusion of field test questions will throw these numbers off a bit. For instance, TAAS Objectives 1–5 might go from questions 1–22 because of two added field test questions. While this will throw off the question count, only 20 questions on Objectives 1–5 count toward your score. So you never have to worry about finding a question concerning Objective 1 on question 32, because it will never appear there.

Think of the Math TAAS as three different tests, with each test requiring different skills. This works to your benefit, since all you need to do is be aware of these changes and prepare for them accordingly.

Jorge: Yes, knowing what awaits you on the test helps you prepare for it.

Ridley: Before I start discussing each TAAS Objective, I want to mention that at the beginning of the test there is a **Formula and Measurement Conversions Chart**. This chart provides a wealth of information in two categories: *geometry*, as the chart provides all the major formulae for finding the area, perimeter, volume, surface area, and circumference of a variety of geometric shapes; and *measurements*, as the table provides metric and standard units of length, weight, mass, volume, and time. If you come to a question that asks about a measurement or geometric formula, check the chart to make sure you are using the proper formula or measurement.

Alexis: That makes sense. I'm not that comfortable with the math anyway, and if I have the opportunity to make sure I'm using the correct formula, I'm definitely going to use it.

Ridley: You got that right. Now, I'll discuss each of the three math sections, and the Objectives that they cover. Is everybody ready now? X!Frumious, how am I doing for time?

> **Strategy**
>
> Use the **Formula and Measurement Conversions Chart** at the front of the test to help you solve questions involving formulas or measurements.

X!Frumious: (mumbled because of something in mouth) Delicious!

Ridley: Okay then, here we go.

The First Third: Concepts (TAAS Questions 1–20)

Ridley: The questions on the first third of the Math TAAS test your ability to understand various mathematical relationships, to identify patterns, to accurately read graphs and charts, to understand measurement concepts, and to make connections among various parts of a numerical relationship. Each question has four answer choices.

TAAS Objective 1: Number Concepts (4 questions)

Ridley: In general, Number Concept questions are centered around such basic concepts as least to greatest, rounding, fractions, decimals, consecutive integers, and other basic math terminology. On recent tests, there has been one scientific notation question and one fractions question.

1. The distance between the Sun and Jupiter is approximately 5.27×10^{11} miles. Which is another way to express this distance?

    A. 0.0000000000527 miles
    B. 0.00000000527 miles
    C. 527,000,000,000 miles
    D. 52,700,000,000,000 miles

Ridley: Now, if you remember what you've learned about scientific notation, you'll be all set. But if you don't remember, what would you do?

Daniel: I would use process of elimination and look at the answer choices. Using common sense, I could rule out choices A and B because there's no way Jupiter and the Sun are that close. If they are, humanity would be in a lot of trouble, as the collision of a gas giant planet and the sun would not be good news for our tiny world. That leaves either C or D.

Ridley: C is the answer, because with scientific notation you take the exponent of 10 (that's the number to right of 10 written in superscript) and move the decimal point that number of spaces to the *right*. So, since it's 10^{11} in this problem, you move the decimal point 11 spaces to the right and get C.

As for a fractions question, don't expect to see something straightforward like "Please convert $\frac{43}{127}$ into a decimal figure." Instead, it might look like this:

2. Kaitlyn surveyed a group of people at the mall and asked each person what his or her favorite sport was. The chart below shows the result of her survey.

Information

In scientific notation, if the exponent (the small number to the right of the 10) is a **negative** number, move the decimal point that many places to the **left**, not right. That way, 3.47×10^{-4} becomes 0.000347.

Which list shows the results in order from greatest interest to least interest?

Favorite Sport	Part of Group Surveyed
Soccer	$\frac{1}{10}$
Football	$\frac{9}{20}$
Basketball	$\frac{1}{5}$
Baseball	$\frac{1}{4}$

A. Soccer, Basketball, Baseball, Football
B. Basketball, Soccer, Football, Baseball
C. Football, Baseball, Basketball, Soccer
D. Football, Basketball, Baseball, Soccer

Ridley: This question is interesting because it combines two different number concepts—fractions and greatest to least. To solve this, let's first look to see which sport is the most popular, and the best way to do this is to find a common denominator for all these fractions.

Information

To find the common denominator (the denominator is the lower half of a fraction), multiply the numerator and denominator of the Soccer fraction by 2, the numerator and denominator of the Basketball fraction by 4, and the numerator and denominator of the Baseball fraction by 5. That way, all the fractions will have a denominator of 20, the common denominator.

Jorge: The fraction $\frac{9}{20}$ is the largest fraction there. So, taking a cue from Daniel, I'll eliminate any answer choice that doesn't start with Football. That leaves C and D.

Ridley: Which one has more fans, Baseball or Basketball? Once we do the math and figure out the answer is Baseball, we can pick answer choice C and move on.

As you work through the test, remember that most of the problems on the Math TAAS are not designed to be straightforward. Some questions may even look really weird, and at first glance you wonder, "What am I supposed to do with this?" This is why there are some students who know everything there is to know about fractions but still do badly on the Math TAAS, because they don't know or are unsure about how to use their knowledge. On the above question, if someone got flustered by the chart format, and all the talk about sports, knowing how to get common denominators would not have mattered. Just make sure to take the time to figure out just what each question is asking.

TAAS Objective 2: Algebraic/Math Relationships and Functions (4 questions)

Ridley: These questions tend to fall into four major categories: patterns, ratios, number lines, and formula questions. Here's what these questions often look like . . .

Jorge: Excuse me, Ridley, but can you be sure that these types of questions will be on the actual test we take?

Ridley: The answer is, "yes and no." "Yes" because the TAAS is a standardized test and therefore can't change too much from one year to the next, or else it couldn't be used for the purpose it was created for. The answer is "no" because each administration of the TAAS is a little different, so there may not be a pattern question on one particular test. However, for the most part the TAAS follows a routine more than it does not. Take the pattern question like the one below.

3. What number should come next in this pattern?

   2, 4, 12, 36, 180, ...

   A. 1,440
   B. 1,260
   C. 1,080
   D. 360

On math questions in the lower grades TAAS tests, pattern questions are almost always solved by adding or subtracting numbers. However, on the Exit-Level Test, these questions are almost always found by multiplying numbers (or dividing, although this is rarer). What this means to you is that the solution to a pattern problem will usually involve multiplication. So in the problem above, you need to figure out how multiplication is used.

X!Frumious: Well, the first number is multiplied by 2, the second number is multiplied by 3, and the one after that by 4. So I need to multiply 180 by 6 to get . . . answer C.

4. The ratio of students to teachers at Middlebrook High is 7 to 4. If there are 28 teachers at the school, how many students are there?

   A. 16
   B. 28
   C. 49
   D. 196

> **Information**
>
> *Solutions to pattern problems usually involve multiplication.*
>
> *With ratio problems, the key is to set up the ratio properly. You will be provided with one complete ratio and will be asked to complete another ratio.*

Daniel: I eliminated B because it was a number that appeared in the question itself. After that, I just guessed C since D seemed too large and A was too small.

X!Frumious: I took the first ratio, $\frac{7}{4}$ and made it equal to the second ratio, $\frac{x}{28}$. Since $\frac{7}{4} = \frac{x}{28}$, the missing number, x, must be 49, answer C.

Ridley: You're both correct.

Number lines are fairly straightforward, so just brush up on your number line skills. Know which side of 0 the negative numbers are on, and how to show that $y > 4$ but also $y < -3$, and you'll be fine. If you had the question:

> 5. Which of the following answer choices best expresses the condition, $-3 \le g < 5$?
>
> A.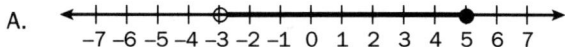
>
> B.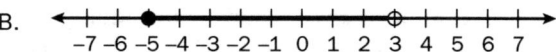
>
> C.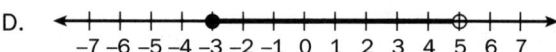
>
> D.

Ridley: Choice A looks good, but remember that g is greater than or *equal to* −3. This means the circle on −3 needs to be darkened in, since that denotes equality. The other side of this condition states that $g < 5$, which means there should be an open circle, not a darkened one. B has the numbers wrong, C has the greater than/less than arrows going in the wrong direction, and only D has the correct number line.

In formula questions, you are provided with a formula with two variables, as well as values for the variables. Your mission, should you choose to accept it, is simply plug in the values for those variables and solve the problem.

6. The total cost of uniforms, *u*, is given by the formula

$$u = 23.50k + 5.60$$

where *k* is the number of uniforms purchased and $5.60 is the service charge. What is the total cost of 7 uniforms?

A. $29.10
B. $164.50
C. $170.10
D. $203.70

If you write everything down, you will have no problem with this question. Just plug in 7 for *k*, giving you $23.50 × 7, and then remember to add the $5.60 service charge. If you don't add the service charge, you get B. The correct answer is C.

TAAS Objective 3: Geometric Properties and Relationships (4 questions)

Ridley: Geometry questions on the test concentrate on problems involving triangles, angles, the occasional (*x*, *y*) grid, and various geometry terms. The Formula Chart in the test can help you on some questions, but on others, the best technique is something you carry with you at all times: *your eyes.*

Strategy

Use your eyes to help you eliminate answer choices on geometry questions. Look at the diagram that accompanies the problem to estimate the correct distance with your eyes.

Be aware, though, that on diagram questions involving angles, the range of answer choices is usually close together, so using your eyes to eliminate choices is not as effective as it is when measuring lines.

7. A building casts a shadow that is 120 feet long. At the same time Gavin, who is 5 feet tall, casts a shadow 8 feet long. How tall is the building?

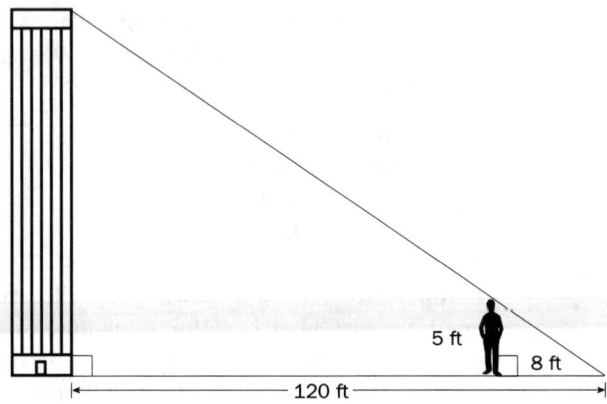

A. 15 feet
B. 24 feet
C. 75 feet
D. 192 feet

Ridley: Some students might believe they have to do the math for this. If you know the math, that's fine, but since the TAAS is a multiple-choice test, there is more than one way to find the answer.

Use your eyes and look at the problem. You will see that the diagram is relatively close to scale. If the shadow is 120 feet long, guess how tall the building might be. Is it about half of the shadow, or more than half?

Willy: I say it's a little more than half.

Ridley: Is it longer than the shadow itself?

Daniel: Definitely not.

Ridley: Well, if it's definitely not longer than the shadow itself, that means it is not longer than 120 feet, and we can cross out choice D. Similarly, if you look at the height of the man, who is 5 feet tall, and then look at the building, you should see that A and B are too small. That leaves C, so C it is. Don't worry about the actual math; the real question throughout the TAAS should not be "How do I do the math?" but "How do I answer the question correctly?"

Using your eyes is the key to solving geometry questions. Barring that, you can always refer to the formulas at the front of the test, but those don't guarantee success. Two more things you should know about the geometry

questions concerns three-dimensional objects and congruency. Congruency is a term often used on the Math TAAS. It is tested in a variety of ways, so just remember that when you see the word *congruency*, it means "same shape and same size." The Exit TAAS also

delights in making sure you know the basic three-dimensional shapes, such as cubes, spheres, pyramids, and cones. Know what these shapes look like blindfolded, and you'll be all right.

TAAS Objective 4: Measurement Concepts (4 questions)

Ridley: Of the four measurement questions, one usually centers around some form of conversion, like changing cups into quarts, or quarts into gallons.

Ridley: Also, be prepared for a volume question, which might state, "what is the volume of . . ." For the most part, though, measurement questions are not that straightforward. Check out the question on the following page.

8. A rectangular park is 110 yards long and $43 \frac{2}{3}$ yards wide. If a person walked all the way around the outside edge of the park, how many yards would he or she walk?

    A. $153 \frac{2}{3}$ yards

    B. $197 \frac{1}{3}$ yards

    C. $263 \frac{2}{3}$ yards

    D. $307 \frac{1}{3}$ yards

Ridley: This question asks us to find the perimeter of a rectangle, but the one word that does not appear in the question is . . . *perimeter*! Here's a perfect example of how the TAAS tests you on an idea, but in an indirect way. This is a perimeter question, and once you figure that out, you just pull up the formula from the front of the test, which is $P = 2(l + w)$, and plug in the numbers from the question.

Daniel: I crossed out choices A and C, because they both had the fraction $\frac{2}{3}$ in them, and that was the exact same fraction that was in the problem.

Ridley: Good use of process of elimination, Dan. If you were unsure of how to proceed on this question, you might look for an answer choice with the same fraction from the problem, but you would be wrong. Now that you've eliminated A and C, you have a 50/50 chance of getting the right answer even if you don't know how to do the math. Sometimes the answer choice will have the same fraction as one of the numbers in the question, so you don't want to do this every time, but it is a good guessing technique.

TAAS Objective 5: Probability and Statistics (4 questions)

Ridley: Under the banner of probability and statistics, expect to see questions about finding an average, in the form of word problems or charts, and probability questions.

9. Jonas bought three shirts at a local clothing store that cost $45.17, $53.24, and $45.17. What was the mean (average) cost of those three shirts?

    A. $45.17
    B. $47.86
    C. $53.24
    D. $143.58

10. For one week, a clothing store kept track of the number of customers it had during the week. What was the mean (average) number of customers for that five-day period?

Monday	140
Tuesday	90
Wednesday	250
Thursday	140
Friday	70

    A. 98
    B. 138
    C. 140
    D. 250

Alexis: Ridley, why is the word *average* in parentheses? And what does *mean* mean?

Ridley: *To find the mean* means to find the average of a group of numbers. To do this, add all the numbers in the group and then divide that sum by however many numbers there are in the group. So, in Question 9, you would add up the prices and divide that sum by 3, since there were three prices.

Willy: So with Question 9, the answer is B, $47.86.

Daniel: I got B also, but I used Process of Elimination. You can cross out A and C because they feature numbers that appeared in the question, and if you think about it, choice D is impossible. I mean, how could the average cost of three shirts exceed the price of each shirt? The average would have to be somewhere between the least expensive shirt and the most expensive shirt, so D is wrong. That leaves B.

Jorge: If I apply Daniel's thinking to Question 10 as well, we can cross out C and D—they both have numbers that appear in the chart. That leaves only A and B, and if I had to guess, I'd pick B because it's closer to the middle of all those numbers, and isn't that what an average is all about?

> **Information**
>
> The most common type of average question on the TAAS is one that asks you to find the mean (average) of a group of numbers. To find the mean, add up the numbers in the group and then divide that sum by however many numbers there are in the group.

Ridley: Smooth work, Jorge. However, if you wanted to do the math on Question 10, it wouldn't be a bad idea. Just add up the five numbers, and then divide by 5. It gets you B as well.

Let's move on to probability questions. One type of probability—one that often includes the phrase *how many different*—usually tests whether you can figure out all the possible combinations of a group of items. To help you solve these questions, get into a multiplying mindset.

11. Auditions for jazz band are currently scheduled for 11:00 a.m., 12:00 p.m., 1:00 p.m., 2:00 p.m. and 3:00 p.m. on Monday, Tuesday, Thursday, and Friday of next week. How many different audition choices (consisting of one time and one day) are available?

   A. 5
   B. 16
   C. 20
   D. 25

To find the whole range of choices, you must multiply the different variables together. In this case, the variables are the times and the days.

Willy: Since there are five audition times, and four days, I would multiply 5 × 4 to get 20, choice C.

Ridley: Correct, Willy. Now, these problems can appear tricky at first, but once you recognize the *how many different* phrase, things should go smoothly, even if I make the question more difficult, like:

> **Strategy**
>
> *When you see a probability question, get into a multiplying mindset.*

12. Auditions for the jazz band are currently scheduled for 11:00 a.m., 12:00 p.m., 1:00 p.m., 2:00 p.m. and 3:00 p.m. on Monday, Tuesday, Thursday, and Friday of next week, and in rooms 234, 256, and 278. How many audition choices (consisting of one time, one day and one room) are available?

    A. 80
    B. 60
    C. 20
    D. 9

Ridley: In the modified question, I've added another variable, the three rooms. Still, you solve the question by multiplying all the variables, in this case 5 × 4 × 3, or five audition times × four days × three rooms = 60.

Strategies: First Third Math

To do well on the first third of the Math TAAS:

Point 1: *Use your eyes when reading diagrams and graphs that measure lines. If the lines look close to scale, you might be able to visually determine the correct answer, or at least eliminate a clearly wrong answer choice. It is more difficult, however, to rely on your eyes for diagram questions involving angles, since the range of those answer choices tends to be closer together.*

Point 2: *With average questions that ask about finding the mean, add up the group of numbers and then divide that sum by however many numbers there are in the group.*

Point 3: *When you see a probability question, think multiplication. On questions that ask about "how many different . . .," you must multiply all the different variables together.*

The Middle Third: Problem Solving
(TAAS Questions 21–44)

Ridley: The questions on the middle third of the Math TAAS each have five multiple-choice answers instead of four. This increase in the number of answers choices is the best way to realize that you've gone from the first section of the test to the middle section. (The change should occur somewhere around the number 21, depending on the field questions.)

The middle third of the test deals with TAAS Objectives 10–13, three of which start with the phrase *Problem Solving Using* . . . Therefore, this section is largely composed of word problems, so be prepared to do reading. This by itself can cause some difficulty, as you find yourself with about four lines of text filled with numbers, and at the end of the question you have no idea what the question wants. The key is to recognize that many of these questions require more than one step of work.

Anyone who tries to work out these problems in his or her head is asking for trouble. Trying to keep track of multiple variables in your head while solving a problem is like juggling with chainsaws: You might be able to get away with it, but if you slip up, the consequences are very painful.

Alexis: But doesn't writing everything down take a lot of time?

Ridley: Not really, and besides, the test is untimed. However, don't spend more than 5–10 minutes on any one problem, because one problem just isn't worth it. Also, if you get into the habit of writing everything down as you problem solve, it doesn't take longer to work a problem on paper than it does to work it in your head. In fact, writing everything down eliminates mental errors.

The biggest difference between the middle third and the first third of the test is that on many word problems, figuring out how to solve the problem is more important than actually finding the answer.

This is somewhat unusual, so you need to understand it. Many of these questions are only interested in determining whether or not you can set up an equation properly. For example:

Prakash went to an arts show. It costs $4.00 to enter the show. While he was there, Prakash spent money for snacks that cost $1.25 per snack. If Prakash spent $10.25 at the show, which equation could be used to find *s*, the number of snacks he bought while there?

A. $4 \times 1.25 \times s = 10.25$

B. $1.25s + 4 = 10.25$

C. $4s + 1.25 + 10.25$

D. $s = \frac{10.25}{(4 + 1.25)}$

E. $s = \frac{10.25}{1.25 + 5}$

Ridley: In the above problem, the test makers aren't interested in finding the actual value of *s*, they just want to see if you know how to find it.

TAAS Objective 10: Problem Solving Using Estimation
(4 questions)

Ridley: Estimation questions are fairly easy to spot, as they usually contain the words *estimating, approximately* or *about*. To solve these questions, round off the numbers in the problem, work the math, and then look at the answer choices.

13. According to a recent poll, about 23% of all students at Brockmorton Junior High School say that they would like to learn astronomy when they go to high school. If there are 815 students at Brockmorton Junior High, which is the best estimate of the number of students who would like to learn astronomy?

A.   25
B.   100
C.   200
D.   250
E.   400

Strategy

Estimation questions often require rounding to the closest whole number. When you round, your total will be reasonably close to the actual amount given in the problem. Make sure you round up or down before you work the math.

Ridley: The key to solving this problem is in understanding that 23% means about one out of four students is interested, and one-fourth of 800 is 200, answer C.

Willy: What if I want to do the math, you know, multiply 0.23 by 815?

Information

Percent means "out of 100."

Therefore, 23% is equal to $\frac{23}{100}$.

Estimate that this is close to $\frac{25}{100}$,

which is $\frac{1}{4}$, or one out of four.

Ridley: You can do that, in which case you'd get 187.45, which you would then round up to 200. However, since you're going to have to do some rounding on every estimation question, it is easier to round *before* you work the math, because 800 divided by 4 is much easier than 0.23 × 815.

TAAS Objective 11: Problem Solving Using Solution Strategies (8 questions)

Ridley: A clearer name for Objective 11 could be "Word Problems That Involve Setting Up a Proportion." Sometimes the proportion is obvious, since it appears in the answer choices.

14. In a nearby neighborhood, 36 out of the 60 residents own dogs as pets. Which proportion could be used to determine d, where d% is the percent of residents who are dog owners?

A. $\frac{60}{d} = \frac{100}{36}$

B. $\frac{60}{36} = \frac{d}{100}$

C. $\frac{d}{36} = \frac{60}{100}$

D. $\frac{36}{60} = \frac{d}{100}$

E. $\frac{d}{60} = \frac{36}{100}$

This is a word problem that doesn't require you to find the answer, it requires only that you set up the equation properly. To do this, keep in mind that every good proportion has two ratios that equal each other, like all the answer choices above. The key is to make sure the two parts of both ratios refer to the same things. For instance, take the first ratio, $\frac{36}{60}$, and label it properly, $\frac{36 \text{ dog owners}}{60 \text{ residents}}$. Now, for the other part of the proportion, we have to use the same labels, $\frac{\text{dog owners}}{\text{residents}}$.

Daniel: Before we do that, though, can I cross out any answer choices that don't have $\frac{36}{60}$, that first proportion, in them?

Ridley: In the real math world, the answer would be "no," because there are other correct ways to write that proportion. However, on the Math TAAS, the answer is "yes," you can cross out any answer choices that do not contain 36 and 60 on the same side.

Daniel: That gets rid of A, C, and E, leaving only B and D. I say it's D.

Ridley: Good guessing. D is correct because the question asks about d, the percent of residents. Since we learned earlier that percent means "out of 100," I know the second proportion will be $\frac{d}{100}$.

X!Frumious: How many proportion questions can we expect to see on the test?

Ridley: Judging from recent tests, four of the eight Objective 11 questions will require you to use proportions in some form or another. The question above was an obvious proportion problem, but others will be harder to spot.

> 15. A nearby desert is 234 miles wide. If the desert is increasing at the rate of 3.5 miles a year, how many years will it take to gain a width of 360 miles?
>
> A. 36 years
> B. 67 years
> C. 103 years
> D. 594 years
> E. 1,260 years

Ridley: This question is tough, so don't be alarmed if the answer isn't obvious. Remember, also, that many of these word problems are multistep questions, requiring more than one calculation. The first thing we need to calculate is, how many miles will the desert need to grow in order to become 360 miles wide?

Willy: $360 - 234 = 126$

Daniel: From here, we could set up the proper proportion, but we can solve the problem just by looking at the answer choices and using common sense.

Strategy

Be sure to label the variables in order to proportion properly.

If the desert has to grow 126 miles, and it's growing at a rate of 3.5 miles a year, choices C, D, and E are all way too much time. A and B are the only possibilities, and I'm guessing A.

Ridley: A is the right answer.

TAAS Objective 12: Problem Solving Using Mathematical Representation (8 questions)

Information

The proper proportion in this case is $\frac{1}{3.5} = \frac{x}{126}$ since this would make

$$\frac{1 \ year}{3.5 \ miles \ of \ growth} = \frac{x \ years}{126 \ miles \ of \ growth}$$

Cross multiply to get

$$3.5 \times x = 1 \times 126, \ or$$
$$3.5x = 126.$$

Then, divide both sides by 3.5 to get $x = 36$.

Ridley: Like objective 11, this objective has eight questions. A more apt name for this objective would be, "Can You Read a Chart?" or a map, or a graph? The majority of these questions will determine how well you can read a map, chart, graph, or Venn diagram.

Venn diagram

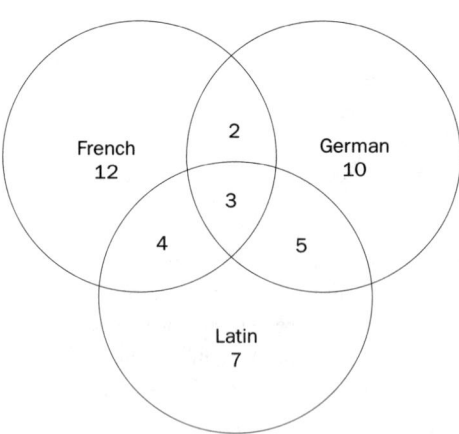

Ridley: A Venn diagram is a series of interlocking circles designed to visually show information. The previous diagram shows how many students at Mythical Junior High are enrolled in various language classes. The numbers inside the circles show how many students are enrolled in each language, as well as how many students are enrolled in one or more languages. That's the advantage of the Venn diagram. For example, to find the number of students who are studying French, you need to add up all the numbers inside the "French" circle.

Daniel: So that would be $12 + 2 + 3 + 4 = 21$.

Ridley: Yes. Since those four numbers are all inside the French circle, that's how many students are taking French classes. But each of those numbers—12, 2, 3, and 4—also means something on its own. You see, the number 12 is inside only one circle, the French circle, so 12 is the number of students who are taking French classes and no other languages. However, the numbers 3 and 4 are also inside the Latin circle, so $3 + 4 = 7$ is the number of students enrolled in *both* French and Latin classes.

Willy: So $2 + 3 = 5$ is the number of students enrolled in both French and German classes.

Alexis: And 3 is the number of students enrolled in all three language classes, since the number 3 is inside all three circles.

Ridley: You're both right. Let's see how you do with a TAAS Venn question.

> O Most Pulchritudinous One, do you remember that Englishman, John Venn, whom we abducted briefly during the mid 20th Century? You know, the one who showed us that cool deal with interlocking circles, and also introduced us to the concept of brunch? That was John Venn.

16. Based on the Venn diagram on the preceding page, how many students are enrolled in more than one language class?

    A.   3
    B.   11
    C.   14
    D.   29
    E.   43

Ridley: To find the answer, add up every number that is inside one or more of the circles. So, $4 + 2 + 5 + 3 = 14$, answer C.

Another prevalent Objective 12 question type is what I call the "Find the Equation" question. These questions ask you to find the equation which can be used to find the value of a certain variable. In fact, the answer choices all contain the variable in them. These are difficult questions, but only if you approach them from a purely algebraic format. Let's look back at an earlier question we saw.

17. Prakash went to an arts show. It costs $4.00 to enter the show. While he was there, Prakash spent money for snacks that cost $1.25 per snack. If Prakash spent $10.25 at the show, which equation could be used to find s, the number of snacks he bought while there?

   A. $4 \times 1.25 \times s = 10.25$

   B. $1.25s + 4 = 10.25$

   C. $4s + 1.25 = 10.25$

   D. $s = \frac{10.25}{(4 + 1.25)}$

   E. $s = \frac{10.25}{1.25 + 5}$

In the Prakash example, we must find the equation that will enable us to find the value of s so we must translate the words of the question into math. To start, Prakash spent $4.00 to enter the show. Then, he spent $1.25 on each snack. Since he bought s snacks, the amount he spent on the snacks was ($1.25 per snack) $\times$ (s snacks), or $1.25s$. So he spent $4.00 to enter the show and $1.25s$ for the snacks. The total he spent was $4.00 + $1.25s$, or $(4.00 + 1.25s)$. We know that he spent a total of $10.25, so the equation for s is $4.00 + 1.25s = 10.25$. This is the same as $1.25s + 4.00 = 10.25$, which is choice B.

TAAS Objective 13: Evaluation of the Reasonableness of a Solution (4 questions)

Ridley: On recent tests, these questions have fallen into two main categories: proportion questions and chart questions. Chart questions provide you with a chart and then ask a question along the lines of "What can be concluded from the information?" These problems are much like

Objective 12 chart and graph problems, and are handled the same way: Make sure to read the chart or graph carefully.

Ridley: The other type of question involves proportions, much like Objective 11 questions, but the answer choices are generally presented as a numerical range. This might look strange at first, but remember that this math section is primarily concerned with whether you know the correct method for solving a question.

18. A catfish swims at a speed of 16 to 17 miles per hour. At this rate, which of these is a reasonable number of miles for a catfish to swim in 3.5 hours?

    A.   Fewer than 20 miles
    B.   Between 30 and 40 miles
    C.   Between 40 and 50 miles
    D.   Between 50 and 60 miles
    E.   More than 60 miles

Here you're given two different rates of speed, but these questions normally require that you set up just one proportion to find the right answer. In this case, $\frac{16 \text{ miles}}{1 \text{ hour}} = \frac{c \text{ miles}}{3.5 \text{ hours}}$. Multiply both sides by 3.5, and you get $c = 56$ miles. Only one answer choice fits that range, so don't worry about the second number, 17 mph.

Daniel The answer, then, is D. This is interesting, because the catfish usually swims at . . .

At this point, O Most Leprous Leader, Ridley's mother showed up with something called "pizza," a circular piece of something that we Kronhorstian's know only as "the gooey red plague." These humans actually pulled off slices and began to ingest it! I'm afraid I fainted in shock and didn't hear the rest of Daniel's sentence.

Strategies: Middle Third Math

Point 1: *With word problems, organize the information in the problem. Label any quantities that are given and identify exactly what you need to find. Then, try to write out the details in the form of an equation or diagram. Make sure to write everything down in front of you—don't problem solve in your head.*

Point 2: *With estimation questions, don't get caught up with finding the precise answer. Round up or down to the closest whole number before you work through the math. Your total will be reasonably close to the actual amount given in the problem.*

Point 3: *With ratio problems, make sure that the numerators and the denominators of all the ratios in the problem refer to the same thing.*

The Final Third: Operations (TAAS Questions 45–60)

TAAS Objective 6: Use of Addition to Solve Problems (4 questions)

TAAS Objective 7: Use of Subtraction to Solve Problems (4 questions)

TAAS Objective 8: Use of Multiplication to Solve Problems (4 questions)

TAAS Objective 9: Use of Division to Solve Problems (4 questions)

Ridley: Of the three math sections, the final third is in some ways the simplest, since every question centers around whether or not you can add, subtract, multiply, or divide correctly. Like the middle third, questions in this section have five answer choices, although the last choice is always "Not Here."

Don't get sloppy and line up the numbers improperly, and don't be in such a rush that you try to do the problem in your head. If a question asks you to add up three numbers with decimals, for example, it is crucial that you do math correctly. If you write everything down, there's a good chance you'll be able to catch a mistake.

Willy: How?

Ridley: Well, if you make a mistake, chances are good you'll get "Not Here" as an answer. Before you pick that answer, you'll want to double check your math, and if you have everything written down, you should be able to spot your mistake.

Some questions in this section are tricky because they are based on converting units such as ounces to pounds, or cups to gallons. Use the **Formula Chart** before attempting difficult conversion questions.

19. Guillermo flew from Anahuac to El Paso and then from El Paso to Brownsville. The flight from Anahuac to El Paso took 7 hours 45 minutes. The flight from El Paso to Brownsville took 8 hours 55 minutes. What was the total flight time from Anahuac to Brownsville?

   A. 15 hours 40 minutes
   B. 16 hours
   C. 16 hours 30 minutes
   D. 16 hours 40 minutes
   E. Not Here

> **Information**
>
> *"Not Here" is the correct answer for one to six questions in this section, so don't be too concerned if you feel you've done the math correctly, but the answer you've come up with is nowhere to be found.*

Ridley: First, add the two flying times to get 15 hours, 100 minutes. But the trick is to remember to convert that number to 16 hours, 40 minutes.

This example is fairly straightforward, because everyone is familiar with converting hours to minutes. However, if there's a question converting quarts to ounces, or yards to miles, or cups to gallons, then you might have some trouble. That's why you should check with the Formula Chart before attempting a question like that.

Regarding use of the process of elimination, remember that POE works well on questions involving fractions. It's not a guarantee, but most of the time if you see a fraction like $\frac{1}{3}$ in a problem, chances are good that an answer choice containing $\frac{1}{3}$ will probably be incorrect.

You should always attempt the math, but if the math stumps you, eliminate answer choices, take an educated guess, and move on.

And that's all for the Math TAAS! X!Frumious, check the stopwatch I gave you. What numbers do you see?

Daniel: (peering over X!Frumious's shoulder) The watch has been mangled somehow, but it still says, "34 minutes, 8 seconds." Exactly as long as you said it would take.

Ridley: Yippee! Hooray! 2, 4, 6, 8, who do we appreciate?

Everyone: Ridley!

Strategies: Final Third Math

Point 1: Many math questions require great precision, so always write down your work, and don't be sloppy. Don't try to solve a problem in your head, no matter how simple you think it is. If you have everything written down, you'll be able to spot your mistake.

Point 2: Refer to the **Formula Chart** at the front of the test to answer questions requiring conversions. Some questions are tricky because they are based on converting units, such as ounces to pounds, or miles to feet, so be sure to use the Chart to help you.

Point 3: Use Process of Elimination on questions involving fractions. If you see a fraction like $\frac{1}{3}$ in a problem, chances are good that an answer choice containing $\frac{1}{3}$ will be incorrect. Always attempt the math, but if the math stumps you, eliminate answer choices, take an educated guess, and move on.

Point 4: If you arrive at a number that is not one of the answer choices, recheck your math. If you get the same number again, choose "Not Here." Keep in mind that up to six questions on this section have "Not Here" as the correct answer.

Sample Questions: Math

Concepts (TAAS Questions 1–20)

1. What volume of water can be kept in an aquarium that is 30 feet long, 22 feet wide, and 8 feet deep?

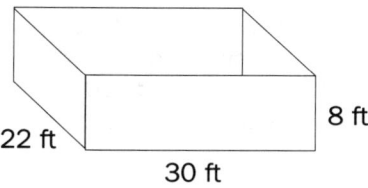

A. 416 cubic feet
B. 660 cubic feet
C. 5,280 cubic feet
D. 15,840 cubic feet

2. The city traffic department set up a system to count the number of cars that passed through the Ash and Main intersection from Monday through Friday. What was the mean (average) number of cars per day for the five-day period?

Day	Number of Cars
Monday	160
Tuesday	160
Wednesday	140
Thursday	220
Friday	240

A. 140
B. 160
C. 184
D. 240

3. On a digital scale, a Fredericksburg peach weighs 0.364 pounds. What is the weight of the peach rounded to the nearest hundredth of a pound?

A. 0.004
B. 0.36
C. 0.367
D. 0.4

4. While at the school store, Markus can choose from the items listed below. How many different choices consisting of 1 pen, 1 notebook, and 1 pencil does he have?

Pens	Notebooks	Pencils
Blue	spiral	plastic
Red	plain	wood
Black		mechanical

A. 3
B. 6
C. 8
D. 18

5. In the figure below, what is the measure of angle q?

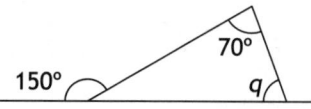

A. 150
B. 80
C. 70
D. 40

6. What number should come next in this pattern?

    1, 2, 2, 4, 8, 32, ...

    A. 16
    B. 64
    C. 126
    D. 256

7. The expression $t(q - w)$ is equivalent to

    A. $tq - tw$
    B. $t - tw$
    C. $t - q - w$
    D. $tq - w$

8. A swimming pool has a filter that processes 6 quarts of water per minute. How many gallons of water does the filter process every hour?

    A. 30 gal
    B. 60 gal
    C. 90 gal
    D. 360 gal

9. Michelle bought a hat on sale at 80% off the regular price of $42. A way to find the amount of money Michelle saved is to multiply $42 by

    A. $\frac{4}{5}$

    B. $\frac{21}{40}$

    C. $\frac{1}{5}$

    D. $\frac{2}{25}$

10. The picture below shows the shadow cast by a tree.

    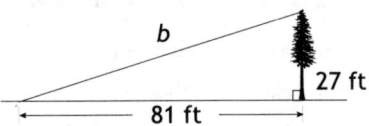

    How long is the line segment b?

    A. between 70 and 80 feet
    B. between 80 and 90 feet
    C. between 90 and 100 feet
    D. between 100 and 110 feet

Problem Solving
(TAAS Questions 21–44)

11. By the shortest route, what is the highway mileage between Elgin and Blanco?

    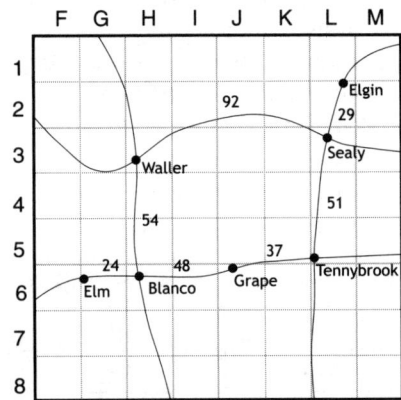

    A. 117 miles
    B. 128 miles
    C. 136 miles
    D. 165 miles
    E. 175 miles

12. The graph below shows the geographic breakdown of the students of Strack High.

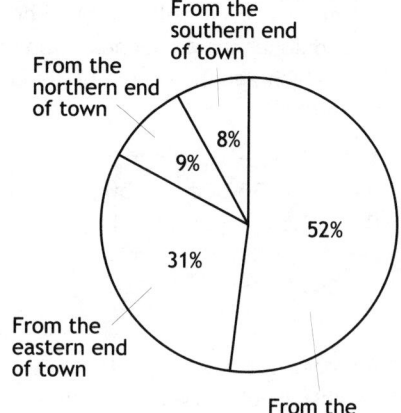

From the southern end of town

From the northern end of town

8%

9%

52%

31%

From the eastern end of town

From the western end of town

Which conclusion can be drawn from the data shown on the graph?

A. Less than half of all students are from the western end of town.

B. More than one-third of all students are from the eastern end of town.

C. Most students are from the eastern or northern part of town.

D. There are more students from the eastern part of town than there are from the western part of town.

E. There are more students from the northern part of town than there are from the southern part of town.

13. According to a recent poll, 43% of the employees at Mike's Gym went to college and received a degree in physical therapy. If there are 89 employees at Mike's Gym, what is the best estimate of the number of employees who are physical therapy graduates?

A. 10
B. 20
C. 40
D. 50
E. 90

14. In Mr. Fischer's homeroom class, 17 out of 32 students are right-handed. Which proportion could be used to determine r, where $r\%$ is the percentage of students who are right-handed?

A. $\frac{17}{32} = \frac{r}{100}$

B. $\frac{32}{r} = \frac{100}{17}$

C. $\frac{32}{17} = \frac{r}{100}$

D. $\frac{r}{32} = \frac{17}{100}$

E. $\frac{r}{17} = \frac{32}{100}$

15. A soft-drink company did a survey to see how many people had drunk their two soft drinks, Jooky and Cajon Lite. The results are shown below.

    R = Set of 400 people surveyed
    J = Set of people who drank Jooky
    C = Set of adults who drank Cajon Lite

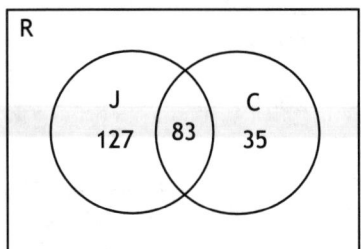

    How many people surveyed had not drunk either soft drink?

    A.   83
    B.   155
    C.   238
    D.   245
    E.   321

16. At Jenkins Brake Repair the minimum salary is $14,200 annually. The maximum salary is $93,500. If j represents an employee's salary in dollars, which of the following best expresses this condition?

    A. $14,200 < j < 93,500$
    B. $14,200 + 93,500 \leq j$
    C. $0 \leq j < 14,200$
    D. $93,500 - 14,200 > j$
    E. $93,500 \geq j \geq 14,200$

17. A basic cable television package costs $36.50 per month. Each additional channel costs $3.50. Lynn's cable bill costs $61 per month. If c represents the number of additional cable channels Lynn has, which equation could be used to find c?

    A. $(36.50 + 3.50)c = 61$
    B. $61 = 36.50c + 3.50$
    C. $36.50 - 3.50c = 61$
    D. $61 = 36.50 - 3.50c$
    E. $36.50 + 3.50c = 61$

18. A grocer has discovered that roughly 1 out of every 7 bushels of lettuce she receives contains a rotten plant. If the grocer receives a shipment of 60 bushels of lettuce, which is a reasonable number of bushels with rotten plants to expect?

    A.   Less than 7
    B.   Between 8 and 9
    C.   Between 9 and 11
    D.   Between 11 and 13
    E.   Between and 14 and 15

19. A post oak is 93 feet tall. If it grows 1.5 feet per year, how many years will it take until the tree reaches 120 feet?

    A.   Just under 2 years
    B.   9 years
    C.   18 years
    D.   27 years
    E.   80 years

20. If 1 marble is selected at random from a bag containing 6 blue marbles, 12 red marbles, 18 green marbles, and 24 black marbles, what is the probability that the marble will be green?

    A. $\frac{1}{12}$

    B. $\frac{1}{6}$

    C. $\frac{3}{10}$

    D. $\frac{1}{3}$

    E. $\frac{5}{12}$

21. Jeb's truck uses $2.18 worth of gas to travel 33 miles. Which is the best estimate of the number of miles Jeb could drive, at the same rate, on $20.00 worth of gas?

    A. 150 miles
    B. 200 miles
    C. 250 miles
    D. 300 miles
    E. 350 miles

22. Monti has to place a length of rope around the outer edge of a well so that no one accidentally falls in. If the well has a diameter of 14 feet, which is the shortest length of rope that will completely encircle the sign?

    (Use $\pi = \frac{22}{7}$)

    A. 44 feet
    B. 33 feet
    C. 22 feet
    D. 14 feet
    E. 7 feet

Operations
(TAAS Questions 45–60)

23. An infant weighs 8 pounds 11 ounces at birth. Two months later, the child had gained 3 pounds 7 ounces. How much did the baby weigh at 1 month?

    A. 11 pounds 2 ounces
    B. 11 pounds 8 ounces
    C. 12 pounds 6 ounces
    D. 12 pounds 8 ounces
    E. Not Here

24. A fishing reel contains 420 feet of fishing line. If Monroe has used $240 \frac{2}{3}$ feet of the line, what is the total number of feet remaining in the fishing reel?

    A. $179 \frac{1}{3}$ ft

    B. $180 \frac{1}{3}$ ft

    C. $200 \frac{2}{3}$ ft

    D. $660 \frac{2}{3}$ ft

    E. Not Here

25. Candace agreed with the car dealership to pay off her car loan of $2,212 in 28 monthly payments. If each payment is the same amount, how much will Candace pay each month?

    A. $27.00
    B. $78.50
    C. $79.35
    D. $92.15
    E. Not Here

26. A recipe for a pot of gumbo calls for $\frac{4}{5}$ cup of okra to make 8 bowls of gumbo. How many cups of okra would be needed to make 10 pots of gumbo?

    A. $\frac{4}{5}$ cup

    B. 8 cups

    C. 10 cups

    D. $12\frac{1}{2}$ cups

    E. Not Here

27. A piece of tape $2\frac{1}{3}$ feet long is needed to close up a packing crate. How many packing crates can be closed up from a roll of tape that is 56 feet long?

    A. 18

    B. $18\frac{1}{3}$

    C. 24

    D. $24\frac{1}{3}$

    E. Not Here

28. Blair works part-time during college as a bicycle courier. He uses his own bike and keeps track of the number of miles he bikes while delivering packages. One week he biked 17.3 miles on Monday, 12.8 miles on Tuesday, 4 miles on Wednesday, and 9.4 miles on Thursday. What was the total number of miles he recorded for that week?

    A. 34.1 miles

    B. 39.5 miles

    C. 42 miles

    D. 42.5 miles

    E. Not Here

29. Linnea bought a new computer. She paid $2,643 for the computer, including $835 for a printer. What was the base price of the computer without the printer?

    A. $1,808

    B. $1,818

    C. $2,559

    D. $3,478

    E. Not Here

30. A chef wants to make $\frac{2}{3}$ of a recipe for wild rice. The recipe calls for 16 pounds of wild rice. How many pounds will the chef need altogether?

    A. 8 pounds

    B. $10\frac{2}{3}$ pounds

    C. $11\frac{1}{3}$ pounds

    D. 24 pounds

    E. Not Here

Reading TAAS

Session Leader: Alexis Wolfe

O Most Truculent Czar of the Galaxy, this meeting took place at Alexis's room. There were books everywhere! Many were on bookshelves, but others were stacked up from the floor to create teetering, six-foot columns of books. At first, I was sure that I was mere moments away from being brained by the Time Life Series: *Gunfighters of the Wild West* set of books balanced precariously near my head, looming like some leather-bound jungle predator in eight easy-to-read volumes. Luckily, no such calamity occurred.

—X!Frumious

NAME: Alexis Antigone Wolfe

BORN: November 27, 1984
Houston, Texas

NOTES: Alexis showed a remarkable ability to read and comprehend at an early stage of life. She finished all the Curious George books by age four, read 10 books of Charles Dickens by age 12, and wrote her first book at age 13, though she has yet to find a publisher willing to print an autobiography of someone who can't even drive. She was voted by classmates as "Most Likely to Write a Thousand-Page Novel While in High School."

Daniel: Alexis, there are books everywhere.

Jorge: Where is the floor? I can't see it. Well, not a lot of it, anyway.

Alexis: Trust me, Jorge, it's there. What else could the books on my floor be resting on? I know many people think I read too much, though I can tell you that such a thing is impossible. There are simply too many good books out there, and no one person could read them all. Speaking of reading, let's talk about the Reading TAAS, shall we?

Alexis: The Reading TAAS has 48 multiple-choice questions with four answer choices each. You will read a passage of text and then answer questions about the passage. There are seven reading passages of approximately 800 words each. Six to eight questions usually follow each passage, though there can be as few as four and as many as nine. Passages are broken down into three main categories:

1. Fiction passages (two-four per test)

2. Nonfiction passages (two-four per test)

3. Oddball passages (zero-three per test)

Overview Reading TAAS

Number of questions	48 multiple-choice questions plus eight field-test questions
Correct answers needed to pass	33 out of 48 questions
Format	seven reading passages, in fiction, non-fiction, or oddball subject. Each reading passage is followed by questions with four answer choices each.
Scoring	Your score is based on the number of questions that you answer correctly. You are not penalized for wrong answers.
Time given for test	untimed

Alexis: On the test, a fiction passage usually tells a story, perhaps about someone our age, and often has an uplifting or inspiring theme. A nonfiction passage is typically educational or instructional, perhaps in the form of a biography or a recollection of a famous event. The third type of passage is what I call an oddball passage, since it comes in a variety of styles: it might be a letter of recommendation, a poster from a play, or even a page from an instruction manual. Despite its unique format, an oddball passage should be treated in the same way that the other passage types are.

Willy: Since the oddball passage is a little different, should we save it for last?

Alexis: Good question, Willy. Work through the reading passages in whatever order you are comfortable with.

The test is untimed, and you're going to answer every question, but that doesn't mean you have to start with question 1 and end with question 48. You've all taken an earlier form of the TAAS before, so you might know if you prefer fiction over nonfiction passages. If you enjoy fiction passages, answer the questions to those passages first, and then move on to the nonfiction passages. Of course, you have to make sure to fill in the proper ovals, since you will be out of sequence, but that shouldn't be hard to do.

Daniel: Do I have to use the passages to decide which order I'll work the questions in?

Alexis: Not at all. You can use the number of questions per passage to determine which passages to work first. For instance, if you have the choice between starting with a shorter passage with nine questions or a longer passage with four questions, you might want to work on the shorter passage first because it will take less time to read and it includes more questions. Remember, the goal on the Reading TAAS is to answer questions, not to read passages, so focus first on those passages that have the most questions. Of course, you'll have to work the longer passage eventually, but let's face it, everyone is fresher at the start of the test, so you might as well use that time to your advantage.

Once you realize that you can work through the problems any way you like, you should gain some confidence in your ability to succeed.

One final note about the passages. In most of our regular school classes, we learn about a topic in class and then take a test to see how well we remember what we have learned. This actually isn't the best way to approach the Reading TAAS.

> **Strategy**
>
> *Don't let unusual reading passages bother you. Except for their different format, oddball passages are just like fiction and non-fiction passages.*

> **Information**
>
> *The Reading TAAS is an open-book test. You do not need to memorize any information in a given passage, since you can refer easily to the text to answer questions. Instead, read the passage to identify the main point and get a good idea of what—and where—the facts are.*

Alexis: If you were to approach the Reading TAAS like your normal school test, you would read a passage, try to memorize as much as possible, and you would answer the questions based on what you had read. Doing this on the Reading TAAS is just a waste time. Instead, read the passage first to understand the main point and get a good idea of what the facts are—and where they are located. Then, answer the questions, but refer to the passage to make sure your answers are correct.

Ridley: What if I look back at the passage but can't find the answer to a question?

Alexis: Then you would try to eliminate some answer choices, take an educated guess, and move on. You need to get only 69 percent of the questions right to get the minimum passing score, so don't panic about any one question, or spend ten minutes trying to answer a hard question.

Jorge: How long should I take on each passage?

Alexis: That depends on how fast a reader you are. Jorge, you've mastered English quite well, but you've had a lot of practice. Other nonnative English speakers might need more time to read a passage, and that's okay. Take whatever time you need to get a general idea of the passage, and then hit the questions. As for the questions, don't spend more than five minutes on any one question, since it's just not worth it. Here are the six question types that you will be tested on.

> **Strategy**
>
> *Take control. You're in charge of the test, not the other way around.*
>
> * *Work through the problems in whatever order **you** are most comfortable with.*
>
> * *If you do answer the questions out of sequence, remember to fill in the proper ovals.*
>
> * *Try working first on the passges that have the most questions. Since you are fresher at the start of the test, you can confidently get more questions out of the way.*

Overview Reading TAAS Objectives

TAAS Objective	Number of Questions on Reading TAAS
1. Word Meaning	4
2. Supporting Ideas	4
3. Summarization	8
4. Relationships and Outcomes	8
5. Inferences and Generalizations	16
6. Point of View, Propaganda, Fact and Nonfact	8

Alexis: Before I discuss each question type, let me provide you with a sample reading passage. I think you'll find it is indicative of the Reading TAAS in its style and content.

The Beautiful Summer Day

"Hey, Margaret, why don't you come play softball with us?" asked Margaret's brother Juan. "It's a beautiful day outside." Juan was standing in the doorway holding his bat and two gloves. Behind him, his friends Ashok and Joey were waiting on the front steps of the house.

Outside the day was bright and sunny, one of the best days in what had been a very hot summer. Yet even though the beautiful day was tempting, Margaret did not feel like going outside. "Thanks, Juan, but I am just not in the mood to play softball right now. You go on."

"Okay, sister, but school's starting soon, and we won't get many more chances to play softball on a Wednesday afternoon. My friends and I will be at Grompton Park if you want to catch up." Juan picked up a baseball cap and left the house.

Margaret watched her younger brother leave and then let out a deep sigh. Juan was right. School was starting soon, and she should be spending the time before her senior year started enjoying herself and having some fun. Unfortunately, Margaret was worried about the upcoming year too much to enjoy herself. In some ways, she was excited about the prospect of applying to college, but at the same time it frightened her. What if she did not get into the college of her choice, or any college at all? Margaret hoped to be a music major in college. She knew she was a very good violinist, but music schools were very competitive, and some of them were also fairly expensive. Margaret's parents would help her out financially as much as they could, but Margaret knew she would have to come up with a portion of the money herself. She had worked at her father's office for the first part of the summer, and had gained a little money that way, but the project she had been working on was finished. Margaret knew she would have to find a job during the school year, and while she had worked and gone to school before, it did not leave her with as much free time as she would have liked.

Margaret went to her room and read for about thirty minutes, but even a book by her favorite author could not help her mood. She went into the study to see if her mother was working on her latest painting, but she was not there. However, there was a slip of paper left on the table addressed to her. Margaret picked up the note and read her Mother's note:

Dear Margaret,

Someone named Teresa called for you this morning while you were in the shower. She asked you to give her a call at 555-8645. I had to go out and buy some more art supplies, but I should be home by 4:30.

The note was a little puzzling to Margaret at first. She had one friend named Teresa, but she lived in Fort Worth, which was over 200 miles away. But since the number Mom wrote down was a local number, that must mean that Teresa was in town. Margaret and Teresa had met during band summer camp two years ago, and quickly became good friends. Teresa was an excellent flute player, and the two of them had even played together on several occasions. Still, Margaret did not go to band summer camp this year, and she had not heard from Teresa in several months.

Margaret dialed the number her Mom had left her. After several rings, a male voice answered, "Hello?"

"Hello, this is Margaret Brantley. May I speak to Teresa?"

"Sure, let me just find her," the man replied. "I think she's in the kitchen with her brother." The line went silent for a while, and then Teresa's voice said, "Margaret? Is that you?"

"It certainly is," she replied. "How are you, Teresa?"

"I'm wonderful!" exclaimed Teresa. "My parents just moved to town, so now I live only a few miles away."

"That's great, Teresa!"

"And there's more," continued Teresa. "My father got the job as the head chef at Bertram's, and they're looking for a group of musicians to play there on the weekends. I asked if I could get the job, and the owner of Bertram's agreed, but only if I could find a quartet. I have a cello player, and a clarinetist, but we need a violinist. Are you interested? It pays very well."

Margaret did not hesitate at all. "You bet I am! What do I need to do?"

Teresa told her. "Our first practice is tomorrow at 10:00. Can you make it?" Margaret told her she could, and Teresa gave Margaret her new address. Then she ended the conversation, claiming that she had to help unpack.

Margaret put the phone down in an <u>exuberant</u> mood. For such a short phone call, it contained a lot of good news. Margaret looked down at her feet and noticed her softball glove lying underneath the kitchen table. She picked it up and headed out the door for Grompton Park. After all, she thought, it would be a shame to waste such a beautiful day.

TAAS Objective 1: Word Meaning (4 questions)

Alexis: Throughout various passages in the reading section, you will see four underlined words. These words, such as <u>quartet</u> in the passage above, will be followed by a question typically phrased like this:

In the passage, the word <u>quartet</u> means—

This is a Word Meaning question, and you must select the answer choice that best defines that word.

> **Strategy**
>
> There are two ways to get the correct answer on a Word Meaning question:
>
> 1. Know the meaning already; or
>
> 2. Figure out the meaning of the word from the sentences around it.

Alexis: To do so, I recommend learning how to figure out the meaning of the word by how it's used in a sentence, also called *context*.

X!Frumious: That sounds kind of hard.

Alexis: It's easy once you get the hang of it. All of you learn words in context. Take the sentence, "Maria feigned being sick so she could stay home from school." If you don't know what *feigned* means, you can still figure it out by looking at the rest of the sentence. It means *faked*.

Here's another example. Suppose we heard a phone ringing and I said, "Could you please pick up that mackinute? I'm expecting an important call." What do I mean by *mackinute*?

Jorge: I believe you intend for it to mean a *telephone*.

Alexis: Exactly! You figured out the word by using the clue words like *pick up* and *important call* to deduce the word's meaning. Try the problem below. Be sure to refer back to **The Beautiful Summer Day** passage.

1. In this passage, the word <u>exuberant</u> means—

    A. spirited
    B. fretful
    C. disillusioned
    D. capable

Alexis: Look at the sentence after *exuberant*, and determine what kind of word *exuberant* could be. Is it going to be a positive or negative type of word?

Ridley: I would assume it stands for something positive, since Margaret just received all that good news.

Alexis: Correct. If we know that *exuberant* is a positive word, we can eliminate choices B and C, both negative words. That leaves A or D, and since Margaret seems happier than efficient, A is the correct choice.

If you like answering Word Meaning questions, here's something you can do during the test. When reading a passage for the first time, if you come across an underlined word, take the time right then to figure out what it means. Then, go straight to the Word Meaning question to answer it.

Daniel: Yeah, why not? I know the underlined word is going to show up in a question, so why not answer the question as soon as I see it.

Ridley: Oh, I don't think that's a good idea for me. I prefer reading the entire passage to get the general idea, then going to the questions. I'm afraid I would lose my train of thought if I left the passage midway through to go answer a question.

Alexis: The choice is yours. Do whatever you are most comfortable with. Of course, Ridley, when you get to the Word Meaning question, go directly to the place it occurs in the passage and reread the sentences around it. I recommend starting two sentences before the underlined word, and reading through until two sentences after it, just to make sure you understand the context.

> **Strategy**
>
> *When you come across an underlined word for the first time, you might want to figure out right away what it means and go straight to the Word Meaning question to answer it. Starting two sentences before the underlined word, and reading through until two sentences after it, use the context of the sentence to determine the word's meaning.*

TAAS Objective 2: Supporting Ideas(4 questions)

Alexis: Supporting Idea questions focus on small facts stated within a reading passage—facts you would probably not remember correctly if you just read the passage once and went on to the questions. Answers to Supporting Idea questions are always directly stated in the passage, so the key here is to refer back to the passage for the answer. Here's an example.

A man in a blue business suit walks into a bank wearing a large green duck on his head. The bank teller looks at him and asks, "Is it hard to keep that thing balanced like that?"

"Not really," replied the duck. "I've got sticky, webbed feet."

Supporting Idea questions related to the above story would be, "What color was the man's suit?" or "What size was the duck?"

Alexis: The main pitfall in Supporting Idea questions is when you *sort of* remember the answer to the question, and an answer choice looks right, so you pick it. But it's wrong! There's no point in trying to answer these questions from memory; it will only hurt your score. Going back to **The Beautiful Summer Day** passage:

O Galactic Uberdude, at first I was as puzzled by this story as you probably are, but then I learned that, unlike us, humans do not usually wear ducks as headgear. (Truly, these humans have no sense of fashion.) Furthermore, I learned the hard way that Earth ducks are not the well-spoken intellectual philosophers that our Kronhorstian ducks are. However, both duck breeds eat bread crumbs when you throw them some.

2. In the story, Margaret's mother was not around because she—

A. went to buy art supplies
B. was in the shower
C. was at Grompton Park
D. went to play softball

Alexis: This is not a central fact in the story, but it is mentioned, and the key is to find where in the passage it is. This is why, when reading a passage for the first time, you try to get a general idea of what events occur when. If you do that well, you'll head straight to the note that says *Mom went to buy art supplies*, and you'll see choice A is correct.

Ridley: Alexis, are there any good elimination techniques to use on this question?

Alexis: Not as many as in other questions, because on one hand the answer is taken directly from the passage. You either find it or you don't. On the other hand, if you read that Juan is at Grompton Park and he's playing softball, you could correctly assume that C and D are incorrect answer choices left there to trap any student who confuses Juan's actions with his mother's activities. But even if you cross out C and D, it's still in your best interest to look for the precise answer, because it will be there somewhere.

> **Strategy**
>
> *Don't try to answer Supporting Ideas questions based on what you think you remember or what looks right. Often, the wrong answers will be "misplaced details"—details taken from different parts of the passage. Make sure you go back and look at the passage for the precise answer.*

TAAS Objective 6: Point of View, Propaganda, Fact and Nonfact (8 questions)

Alexis: I placed TAAS Objective 6 with Objectives 1 and 2 because all of these question types have answers that can be found directly in the passage. The answers to Word Meaning, Supporting Idea, and Fact vs. Nonfact questions can all be lifted straight from the passage, as opposed to the other three questions types, which are not as direct.

Now there are eight questions that fall under the cumbersome title, **Point of View, Propaganda, Fact and Nonfact**, but half of them simply ask, "Which is a FACT in the passage?" Elimination is a good

> **Information**
>
> *16 of the 48 reading questions (or one out of three) have answers that can be found directly in the passage. This is good news, as it means that all you need to do is to determine where the information can be found.*

technique here because there are usually one or two answer choices that can be crossed out immediately. You see, wrong answer choices on the FACT questions contain words that express an OPINION, something that cannot be proven. These answer choices use words like *excited*, *easier*, *faster*, *enjoys*, *superior*, *unlucky*, *thinks*, and *courageous*. Even though most people believe that "eating a cracker is easier than scaling Mt. Everest in a bathrobe," that doesn't make it a fact, because there is no way to conclusively prove it.

Look at the statements below, and decide which are facts and which are opinions.

1. Michael Jordan was the greatest basketball player ever.

2. Michael Jordan was a great basketball player.

3. Michael Jordan won multiple NBA scoring titles.

4. Michael Jordan won a whole bunch of NBA scoring titles.

5. Michael Jordan has appeared in a movie.

6. Michael Jordan is the greatest actor ever.

Daniel: Well, I feel fairly certain that statement #6 is not a fact.

Jorge: #1 seems too extreme to be a fact, but #2 is more reasonable.

Alexis: Yes, but both #1 and #2 are opinions, not facts. You can't go into a laboratory and prove that someone is "great." However, #3 can be proved, since Jordan won the scoring title at least five times that I know of. On the other hand, #4 can't be proved, because you can't define exactly what "a whole bunch of" is. And #5 is a fact, since it can be shown that Jordan was in a movie, but as for #6 . . . I agree with Daniel on that one.

So, let's try a question related to **The Beautiful Summer Day** passage.

3. Which is a FACT in the passage?
   A. Margaret will enter college next year.
   B. Juan's two best friends are Ashok and Joey.
   C. Margaret is a very good violinist.
   D. Juan leaves to play softball.

Alexis: The first incorrect answer choice you might spot is C, since the word *good* is open to interpretation, and therefore not a fact. I eliminated B as well, since it is not stated that those two are best friends, and the word *best* makes this statement hard to prove. That gets rid of two choices, giving us a 50/50 shot. The answer is D, since there's no way to prove A as a fact. Margaret wants to go college next year, but she doesn't mean she *will* go to college.

Daniel: On these FACT questions, it seems that you use elimination to get rid of everything but the answer.

Alexis: True, since only one answer choice will be factual.

Sometimes the test has one "Which is an OPINION in this passage?" question. Answer this the opposite way; look for the answer choice that is subjective, and eliminate any choices that are facts that can be proved in the passage.

> ### *Strategy*
>
> *Use POE for FACT questions. Look for, and eliminate, incorrect answer choices that express an opinion— something that cannot be conclusively proven. Work through the answer choices one by one until you are left with the one factual statement.*

TAAS Objective 3: Summarization (8 questions)

Alexis: I started this study group by saying you should first read a passage to get the main idea. Not only will this help you comprehend the passage better, it will also help you to answer Summarization questions. Five or six of these Summarization questions will ask "What is the main idea of this passage?" or "What is the best summary of this passage?" To answer these questions, first figure out what the big picture, or main idea, of the passage is. Then, with that big picture in mind, look for the *positive* answer choice.

When trying to identify the big picture of a passage, it

> ### *Strategy*
>
> *To answer a Summarization question, read the passage and state the main idea, or big picture, in your own words. Then, look for the answer choice that a) captures that main idea and b) is positive and uplifting. Remember, the correct answer choice should not focus on details in the passage.*

helps to understand the individuals who wrote the passage in the first place. The people who write the Reading TAAS passages are educational writers who try to write positive, character-building stories for tenth-graders. Therefore, you are not likely to see a fiction passage discussing gambling addiction or teenagers dying overseas in a senseless, foreign war. Instead, the test includes uplifting biographies of inspirational people as well as stories about students our age who overcome obstacles and become better people for it. So when you go to answer the question, pay close attention to the most positive-sounding answer choices, as they will almost always be a good choice for the correct answer. To demonstrate, let's look at a question from a passage none of us have seen.

4. What is the best summary of this passage?

    A. Joy and her mother use a wooden cage baited with chicken to catch a large opossum.

    B. Despite the difficulties presented by Morris, Joy and her mother decide to still pick berries in the nearby field.

    C. Joy believes the large and cunning Morris may be the same opossum that Joy's mother once tried to catch.

    D. Although their efforts to catch the opossum fail, Joy develops a deep respect for the animal and gains more respect for her mother's spirit and endurance.

Alexis: We know nothing about the passage itself, but we do know about the writers of the Reading TAAS, so here's how to answer this question. First, choice A might be a fact from the passage, but it's not very positive nor does it seem to be a main idea, so we can eliminate it. B could be the main idea, but it seems only slightly broader in scope than choice A. Choice C, like A, might be a fact from the passage, and there's nothing very positive about it, is there? D, however, has a nice, mushy ending that communicates a broad, inspiring message. It's the correct response.

Hopefully, you already recognized at the start that the main idea of the passage

Information

Small facts are often placed as wrong answer choices on Summarization questions, since students recognize them as correct facts. While they may be accurate, they are not the main idea of the passage. To identify the main idea, read the passage and state in your own words what it is about—what point is the author trying to make?

had something to do with Joy and her mom sharing a bonding experience, which would make D all the more obvious a choice. The key to identifying the main idea is to read the passage and state in your own words what it is about. However, even without that, we guessed and got the question right.

Now let's try a question from **The Beautiful Summer Day** passage.

> 5. What is the best summary of this passage?
>
>   A. Margaret's chances of attending college improve after she receives a job offer, leading her to regain her optimism about the future.
>
>   B. Margaret's ability as a musician leads a local restaurant manager to ask her to play at the restaurant.
>
>   C. Margaret knows she will have to do well in school in order to succeed in her goal of going to college.
>
>   D. Worried about having a lack of funds, Margaret initially turns down her brother's offer to play softball at the park.

Jorge: Well, B is not even accurate, so it should go. C and D are both true, but there's nothing really positive about either one, so I picked Choice A, which is uplifting. Also, I felt that the point of the passage was something like, "Margaret starts out bumming that she doesn't have a job, but then gets in a good mood because her friend lands her one." Choice A is a good paraphrase of that idea.

Alexis: Correct! In addition to the Summarization questions, there will also be a couple of questions that ask about the main idea of a smaller chunk of a passage—one or two specific paragraphs. Solve these questions the same way; identify the main point of that paragraph, and look for the positive answer choice.

TAAS Objective 4: Relationships and Outcome
(8 questions)

Alexis: Relationship and Outcome questions ask you to draw a conclusion based on information you have read. The answers to these questions cannot be found directly in the passage, so while you still want to use the text for important information, don't expect the answer to be obvious. Look at the difference between the two questions below:

Supporting Ideas question:

6. In the story, Margaret's mother was not around because she—

    A. went to buy art supplies
    B. was in the shower
    C. was at Grompton Park
    D. went to play softball

Relationships and Outcomes question on the same topic:

7. When Margaret's mother left the house, the place that she will most likely visit is—

    A. Grompton Park
    B. Teresa's house
    C. Bertram's Restaurant
    D. a painting and crafts store

Alexis: Since Relationship questions don't ask for information directly spelled out in the passage, they often contain words and phrases like *most likely*, *probably*, *might*, or *suggests*. In Question 7 above, there is no way to know where Margaret's mother will go, so the question must contain the phrase *will most likely*.

Information

Relationship questions ask you to draw conclusions based on information you have read. Look for clues in the exact wording of the question to help you narrow in on the answer.

Think of these questions as two-step questions. First, find the clue, and then, apply it to the answer choices to find the right response. In **The Beautiful Summer Day**, Margaret's mom doesn't say where she is going, but she leaves the house to go buy art supplies. If we know she needs art supplies (Step 1), (Step 2) will be to pick the appropriate answer choice.

Daniel: That would be D, since you can most likely buy art supplies at a painting and crafts store.

Alexis: That's correct. So while these questions might take a little more effort, they are not necessarily harder. In fact, you can still use

Process of Elimination (POE) on them. Just keep in mind that the people who write the reading passages and questions often lean toward the positive, uplifting side. Here's another question.

8. The author of this passage suggests that the writings and accomplishments of W. E. B. Du Bois will probably be—

A. awarded national honors
B. not very useful to future scholars of African-American history
C. meaningful to future generations
D. disregarded by modern human rights organizations

Daniel: I would get rid of B and D, since they are both negative.

Alexis: That leaves A and C, and from there it's a 50/50 guess unless you look back at the passage. Of course, since there is no passage, I would pick C, since this answer is broader in scope and therefore much harder to disprove.

TAAS Objective 5: Inferences and Generalizations (16 questions)

Alexis: With 16 questions of this type, Inference questions make up one-third of the Reading TAAS. Inference and Generalization is kind of a catch-all category. These questions are a lot like Relationship questions: While the answer is not directly stated in the passage, the clue for finding it is. In fact, many Inference questions use phrases like *provides evidence*, or *gives you reason to believe*.

9. The author of this passage gives you reason to believe that Margaret—

A. enjoys playing the violin
B. has many friends her own age
C. is still working for her father
D. plays softball with her brother every week

Strategy

On Inference questions, the answer is not directly stated in the passage. Look for clues in the question, such as the words *provides evidence* or *gives you reason to believe.*

In this **Beautiful Summer Day** question, it's easier to find all the incorrect answers instead of the one correct answer. We know that Teresa is Margaret's friend, but that doesn't mean *many*, so B is out. And while Juan asks Margaret to play softball one time, there is nothing that states this is a weekly occurrence, so D is out. C is wrong because the passage states that Margaret is no longer working at Pop's office. That leaves A, which I'll pick.

Information

Parts of the passage suggest that Margaret enjoys playing the violin. There's the fact she wants to be a music major, and her readiness to play violin with Teresa at the restaurant.

About 4 of the 16 Inference questions will ask you to determine the emotional state of the author or one of the characters. These questions look like the one below, also from **The Beautiful Summer Day** passage.

10. In the first paragraph, the author establishes a mood of—

    A. anxiety
    B. remorse
    C. anger
    D. anticipation

Alexis: On questions like these, about 75 percent of the time the answer will be a positive one, which means B and C are unlikely to be correct. Since the writers of these TAAS passages are using positive, uplifting themes, there's little room for characters who are vicious, hateful, or irrational. Therefore, if you had a question with the following answer choices, picking choice D is a safe bet.

    A. vicious
    B. hateful
    C. irrational
    D. agreeable

Information

On questions that ask you about the author or character's emotional state, look for the positive answer choice. Most of the time, that will be the correct answer. Just be sure to check your answer choice with the information in the passage.

Alexis: Even though this is the pattern, it still helps to check your work with the passage. Consider the Margaret passage. She isn't really in a good mood when the story begins. So if a question asked you to describe Margaret's mood at the beginning of the story, you wouldn't be looking for a positive answer. The answer to question 10, therefore, is A, since Margaret is anxious about her future. So it pays to check with the passage, but bear in mind that most of the time the broad, uplifting choice is correct.

That's all I have to say about the Reading TAAS. Now, let's move on to more important business. Who has a date to the Spring Ball?

Overview: Reading TAAS Strategies

Strategy 1: *Take control. The Reading TAAS is an open-book test, so there is no need to memorize anything.*

Strategy 2: *As you work through a reading passage, ask, "What is the author trying to communicate?" Make notes about what and where details are.*

Strategy 3: *Work through the problems in whatever order you are most comfortable with. If you do answer the questions out of sequence, though, don't forget to fill in the proper ovals.*

Strategy 4: *Focus first on the reading passages that have the most questions. Since you are fresher at the start of the test, you'll get more questions out of the way.*

Strategy 5: *If you don't know the meaning of an underlined word, try to define it by its context, that is, the meaning of the words and sentences around it.*

Strategy 6: *When identifying the main point of a reading passage, look for a broad, positive-sounding answer.*

Strategy 7: *When asked to draw conclusions about information that appears in a passage, examine carefully how the question is phrased.*

Sample Questions: Reading

W. E. B. Du Bois

In 1895, twenty-seven-year-old W. E. B. Du Bois received his doctorate of philosophy from Harvard University, and thereby became the first African-American to gain a graduate degree from America's oldest university. The Ph.D. was merely one achievement of Du Bois's distinguished academic career, but Du Bois is not known merely for being a good teacher and scholar. Along with Booker T. Washington, W. E. B. Du Bois was one of the most influential African American figures of the early 20th century, working throughout his life to help put an end to racism and prejudice in the United States.

William Edward Burghardt Du Bois was born in 1868 in the small rural Massachusetts town of Great Barrington. Du Bois quickly showed himself to be an eager, apt student, earning high marks in all of his classes. Du Bois longed to go to Harvard, but his application was not accepted. Still resolved to go to college, Du Bois worked for a year after graduating high school to earn money, and four townsfolk—including the school principal—pitched in enough money to send Du Bois to Fisk University, a prominent African American university in Tennessee. After graduating with honors from Fisk, Du Bois applied to Harvard again and was accepted. Although Harvard did not recognize his degree from Fisk, it did provide him with a grant.

After receiving his doctorate from Harvard, Du Bois eventually settled into a job as a professor at Atlanta University. While working there from 1897 to 1910, Du Bois produced his most influential piece of literature, The Souls of Black Folk. *Published in 1903, the novel frankly discusses the challenges involved with eliminating "the color line" in the United States, and critics and scholars alike instantly praised the book for its insight and candor. Du Bois went on to write more than 20 books in his life, both fiction and nonfiction.*

Du Bois did more than write books, however. Two years after The Souls of Black Folk *came out, he founded the Niagara Movement, an early equal rights movement. While the Niagara Movement floundered after a few years, Du Bois joined together with other equal-rights supporters to create the National Association for the Advancement of Colored People, or NAACP, in 1910. The NAACP remains an important social rights organization to this day.*

While at the NAACP, Du Bois became the editor of the organization's magazine, The Crisis. *This magazine reached only a thousand readers in its first year of existence, but its impassioned writing and unique position—it was one of the only magazines to focus on African-American issues—quickly caused its readership level to soar. Within a decade of its founding,* The Crisis *was read by over 100,000 readers, and through this magazine the NAACP was able effectively to pass on its ideals and beliefs.*

Du Bois was one of the foremost African American figures of the early 20th century, but he was by no means the only one. Booker T. Washington, founder of the Tuskegee Institute, was also a prominent character in the equality movement. While both men were deeply committed to improving the lives of African Americans in the United States, they had widely different beliefs. Du Bois believed that African Americans should speak out against prejudice whenever it occurred, and that the fight for equality would be led by college-educated African Americans. Washington, on the other hand, believed that economic independence was the key factor in the push towards equality, and that until economic disadvantages plaguing African Americans were eliminated, racial demands should not be pressed. This disagreement in philosophies caused both Du Bois and Washington to oppose each other's efforts often. Du Bois wrote several essay criticizing Washington and his beliefs, and Washington responded with attacks against Du Bois.

In 1934, Du Bois left as editor of The Crisis *and went back to teaching at Atlanta University. While he returned to the NAACP briefly in the 1940s, Du Bois left the United States in 1961 and went to Ghana, where the president of that country had asked him to compile a massive history of Africa. Du Bois died two years later, and was buried with honors in Ghana. The day after his death, Martin Luther King Jr. gave his famous, "I have a dream" speech, a speech that helped push forward the civil rights movement that Du Bois worked all his life to bring about.*

1. Which is a FACT from the passage?

   A. Du Bois was a courageous fighter for human rights.
   B. Du Bois's first published book was *The Souls of Black Folk.*
   C. The creation of the Niagara Movement was crucial to the success of the NAACP.
   D. Du Bois graduated from Fisk University with honors.

2. The author of this passage suggests that the writings and accomplishments of W.E.B. Du Bois will probably be—

   A. awarded national honors.
   B. not very useful to future scholars of African-American history.
   C. meaningful to future generations.
   D. disregarded by modern human rights organizations.

3. The author of the passage provides evidence to suggest that *The Crisis* became a successful magazine because—

   A. it was one of the only magazines to discuss topics relevant to African-Americans at the time.
   B. the NAACP was new, and people were interested in its creation.
   C. Du Bois already had a large following who read all his works.
   D. it was read by over a 100,000 people a decade after its founding.

4. What is the main idea of this passage?

   A. Du Bois was a well-known scholar while at Harvard.
   B. Du Bois and his work on *Crisis* helped make the NAACP an important organization.
   C. Du Bois worked throughout his life to promote racial equality.
   D. Washington and Du Bois did not often agree with each other.

5. Du Bois believed that future leaders of the African-American equality movement would be—

   A. armed with useful job skills.
   B. well-educated.
   C. members of the NAACP.
   D. authors.

6. The author of the passage provides evidence to suggest that Booker Washington—

   A. worked closely with Du Bois to achieve similar goals.
   B. did not approve of the creation of the NAACP.
   C. was a distinguished scholar like Du Bois.
   D. emphasized learning job skills as a key to improving the lives of African-Americans.

7. Which event in the passage happened last?

   A. *The Souls of Black Folk* is released.
   B. Du Bois works on the history of Africa.
   C. Du Bois goes back to work for the NAACP.
   D. Du Bois teaches at Atlanta University.

The Panama Canal

In 1517, the Portuguese explorer Vasco Nuñez de Balboa crossed the narrow strip of land in Central America separating the Atlantic and Pacific Oceans, and became the first European to see the Pacific. He had sailed across the Atlantic looking for a water passage to China and the Far East, but was unable to find a waterway connecting the two oceans. Had Balboa's distant relatives attempted the same voyage four hundred years later, they would have been successful, thanks to the creation of the Panama Canal in 1914.

Extending just over 50 miles, the Panama Canal is a waterway that connects Limon Bay, in the Atlantic Ocean, to the Bay of Panama, on the Pacific side. The canal allows ships to bypass sailing around all of South America, cutting about 7,800 miles off the typical voyage. Since it is such a time-saving measure, about 13,000 ships use the Panama Canal each year, carrying huge amounts of cargo. Although the canal is still used by many ships, today's oil supertankers are too big to use the canal, and its military use has been limited due to the fact that today's large aircraft carriers are also unable to fit through the canal.

Like the Great Wall of China, the Panama Canal is one of the world's great feats of engineering. However, achieving such an <u>arduous</u> task did not come easily, and many early attempts failed badly. The first attempt to create a transoceanic canal came in 1878, when Frenchman Lucien Napoleon Bonaparte Wyse received permission from Colombia to build a canal across Panama. (At the time, Panama was a territory of Colombia.) Wyse gave his construction rights over to another Frenchman, Ferdinand De Lesseps, whose company had worked on the Suez Canal in Egypt. Lesseps's company started digging in 1882, but soon encountered a host of problems. The group did not have the proper digging tools and dishonest politicians stole vast amounts of money that was supposed to be used towards the building effort. To make matters worse, tropical diseases, such as malaria and yellow fever, killed hundreds of workers. Seven years after it started digging, Lesseps's company went bankrupt.

During the Spanish-American War of 1898, an American warship on the West Coast had to take the long journey around South America in order to bolster the Atlantic Fleet. This delayed journey helped convince the United States Congress that the creation of a canal would be important for national defense. By 1904, the United States gained control of the building rights to the Panama Canal. The United States achieved this by backing Panama's push for independence. In return for America's support, Panama gave the United States exclusive control of a 10-mile strip of land.

Once work on the canal resumed, the most important person was not an engineer, but a physician. Doctor William Gorgas, an American colonel, spent the first two years instituting methods to help eliminate tropical disease from the area. Since diseases such as malaria are carried by mosquitoes, Gorgas made workers drain the swamps where mosquitoes bred and clear away large patches of brush and grass where they swarmed. He also led a program to exterminate rats, which are carriers of bubonic plague. By reducing the disease rate, work on the canal could proceed at a better pace.

Ten years after the United States began work on the project, the Panama Canal was complete. A landslide closed the canal briefly in 1915-1916, but since then the canal has *functioned without interruption. Although the United States was granted exclusive control of the Panama Canal in 1904, soon after it was built the United States and Panama started negotiating over control of the canal. The two sides were at an <u>impasse</u> for many years, but in 1977, the two governments agreed on a treaty that would give control of the land around the Panama Canal back to Panama in 1979. The agreement also stated that canal operations would be handed over to the Panamanian government on December 31, 1999.*

Today, work still continues on the Panama Canal, as various areas are widened to allow more ships through at the same time. If Balboa were to sail from Portugal in search of China today, he could look over the side of his ship as it passes from the Atlantic Ocean to the Pacific Ocean and view the progress himself.

8. The word <u>arduous</u> in this passage means—

   A. gigantic
   B. simple
   C. impossible
   D. difficult

9. What is the main idea of this passage?

   A. The Panama Canal was difficult to build because of many tropical diseases.
   B. The Panama Canal took a long time to complete but has since been very useful.
   C. The independence of Panama helped the United States build the canal.
   D. Most great feats of engineering take a long time to complete.

10. In the passage, the word <u>impasse</u> means—

    A. deadlock
    B. state of confusion
    C. agreement
    D. state of hostility

11. Dr. William Gorgas can best be described as—

    A. hopeful.
    B. ingenious.
    C. calm.
    D. thrifty.

12. Which is an OPINION in this passage?

    A. The Panama Canal connects Limon Bay to the Bay of Panama.
    B. Many canal workers died because of tropical diseases.
    C. Balboa would be surprised to see how his idea of the canal became a reality.
    D. Improvements are still being made to the Panama Canal.

13. While working on the Panama Canal, Ferdinand De Lesseps most likely—

    A. experienced great frustration
    B. gained enormous wealth
    C. achieved international respect
    D. sacrificed personal relationships

14. The passage suggests that during the 21st century the operation of the canal will be in the hands of—

    A. the United States
    B. Colombia
    C. France
    D. Panama

The Fine Arts Fair

Lana carried her painting out of her house and gently placed it in the back seat of her parents car. Today was the day of the Throckmorton Fine Arts Fair, and it was the first year Lana had entered a painting into the competition. Most of the people who went to the show were merely curious, but there were several people who bought one or two paintings every year. Even more importantly, a group of art professors from Rice University awarded one painter and one sculptor each the title of "Top New Artist of the Year." While the honor itself was worth the entry fee of five dollars, the winners of the award would each receive one free art class over the summer at the University of Paris.

Her heart was racing as Lana glanced down at the program sheet to see the schedule of events.

23rd Annual Throckmorton Fine Arts Fair
Sponsored by the Throckmorton Arts Department
March 22, 2000

Location: Busy Bee Garden Complex, 505 Busy Bee Boulevard.

Time: Fair opens at 9:00 a.m. to the public. Contestants displaying their art should arrive 30 minutes before the gates open. The fair will close at 4:00 p.m.

Artwork: Sculptures will be on display at the east lawn of the complex. Paintings will be displayed in both the Merriweather Room and the Phlox Room.

Food: Refreshments will be served at the concession stand near the east lawn. At noon, lunch will be provided by Artz House of Barbecue. Lunch is free for all artists with pieces on display, and $3.00 for everyone else. Visitors are asked not to take any food or drink inside the complex.

Directions: Starting at Throckmorton High School, take the Mulberry Highway west until the Bluebonnet Trail exit. Turn left onto Bluebonnet Trail, and then turn right at Busy Bee Boulevard, which is the third stop light after leaving the highway. (The streets that you will pass after you exit the highway are Granger and Musth, in that order.)

15. Which is the best summary of the program sheet?

    A. It gives the time the fair opens.
    B. It provides directions to the site of the fair.
    C. It gives details about where the artwork is displayed and other necessary information.
    D. It provides a detailed discussion of what foods will be served.

16. The passage gives you reason to believe that the Throckmorton Fine Arts Fair—

    A. has been going on since 1968.
    B. is very close to the high school.
    C. is one of the largest art fairs in the area.
    D. has always been held at the Busy Bee Garden Complex.

17. According to the program sheet, where will Lana's painting be placed?

    A. The east lawn of the complex.
    B. The Merriweather Room.
    C. The Merriweather or the Phlox Room.
    D. The Phlox Room.

18. If Lana arrives at the fair at 9:30, then she will be—

    A. thirty minutes late.
    B. one hour late.
    C. two hours early for lunch.
    D. right on time.

19. Which of these best describes Lana?

    A. nervous but excited.
    B. agitated and frightful.
    C. anxious and pessimistic.
    D. enthusiastic and arrogant.

20. Which of these is a FACT given in the passage?

    A. Lunch will cost Lana $3.00.
    B. Granger and Musth streets intersect each other.
    C. Sculptures may be seen in the Phlox Room.
    D. To get from the garden complex to the high school, at some point you could drive on Bluebonnet Trail and then take the Mulberry Highway east.

Writing TAAS Part 1

Session Leader: Jorge Benitez

> O Great Smelter of All Things Good, our fourth meeting was held in the board room of a health spa that Jorge's parents own. During our meeting, the Mayor called Jorge just to chat. Jorge made him wait for about six minutes, and when he finally did talk to him, it was on speakerphone! Such pluck!
>
> —X!Frumious

NAME: Jorge Estaban Benitez

BORN: May 5, 1984
Oaxaca, Mexico

NOTES: The son of Mexican diplomats, Jorge lived in Greece, Andorra, Thailand, and Malawi before moving to Texas. He is fluent in several languages, including Greek, Catalan, and Thai. Jorge was elected Student Council President by over 80 percent of the student body, but he turned down the position, claiming a life of politics was not his thing.

Jorge: The Writing TAAS has two parts: Part 1 is a 40-question multiple-choice test covering various grammar, spelling, capitalization, and punctuation rules. Part 2 provides you with a statement, and you are asked to agree or disagree in essay format. Your essay is graded on a scale from 1 to 4, with 4 being the highest score. 2 is the minimum passing score for the essay.

X!Frumious: So even if you get all 40 grammar questions right, if you receive a score of 1 on the essay, you have to take the Writing TAAS over again.

Jorge: True, but beyond that, the scores for both parts of the Writing TAAS are linked in the following way: The higher the score you receive on the essay, the lower your score needs to be on the 40-question grammar part, and vice versa.

If you want to look at the chart another way, if you get 30 of 40 grammar questions correct, then you have only to write an essay worth a score of 2. Of course, the problem with this linked-score system is that you don't get to find out your grammar score before you have to write the essay. You have no idea how well you fared on either section until the entire Writing TAAS is over and both sections are graded. So aim for over a score of 27 on the grammar part, and for at least a 2 on the essay, and you will give yourself the best chance of passing.

Overview: Writing TAAS

Format

Part 1	40 multiple-choice questions on grammar, spelling, capitalization and punctuation
Part 2	written essay (composition)

Scoring

The scores for Parts 1 and 2 are interdependent. The better you do on the essay, the fewer multiple-choice questions you need to get right, and vice versa.

Part 1:
Multiple-Choice Questions

If your essay score is 4,
7 out of 40 questions must be answered correctly.
If your essay score is 3,
17 out of 40 questions must be answered correctly.
If your essay score is 2,
27 out of 40 questions must be answered correctly.

Part 2:
Essay

Graded scale from 1 to 4;
2 is the minimum passing score.

Time given for test

untimed

X!Frumious: So I have to get about 67 percent of the grammar questions right. I can still miss 13 questions and get a passing score.

Jorge: Part 1 is divided into three sections. Each section tests a different TAAS Writing Objective, and each one has a different question format. Here's how the question numbers relate to the TAAS Objectives:

Overview: Writing TAAS Objectives

Question Number on Writing TAAS		TAAS Objective	
Part 1:	Questions 1–12	Objective 6:	Usage
Part 1:	Questions 13–26	Objective 7:	Spelling, Capitalization, & Punctuation
Part 1:	Questions 27–40	Objective 5:	Sentence Construction
Part 2:	Essay/Composition	Objective 1-4:	Writing Skills

The First Third: Usage (Questions 1–12)

Jorge: The first 12 questions are primarily fill-in-the-blank questions. There will be two boxed-in passages containing 6–10 related sentences. Six of those sentences will be missing key verbs, pronouns, adjectives, and adverbs. Here is an example:

Why is learning history an important part of school? Historians _____ (1) that without knowledge of past events, people _____ (2) to make the same mistakes over and over again. Some historians would even say that learning history is the _____ (3) thing a person will ever learn. Of course, there is a small group of people who believe that history is completely useless, but _____ (4) are a very small minority of the population.

Since history _____ (5) an exact science, it is often grouped with English, philosophy, art, psychology, and other inexact areas of learning. This different branches of study are often called "The Humanities," and they are taught at almost all universities. Many students find _____ (6) areas of study contain the classes they enjoy the most.

1. A. argue
    B. argues
    C. have argue
    D. will have argued

2. A. continues
    B. will be continuing
    C. will continue
    D. will have continued

3. A. important
    B. most important
    C. more importantly
    D. importantest

4. A. it
    B. you
    C. we
    D. they

5. A. isn't
    B. is not hardly
    C. aren't never scarcely
    D. isn't never

6. A. them
    B. this
    C. these
    D. their

Jorge: While most people do a good job of speaking English, these same people think that they do not know proper grammar. It is as if the word *grammar* conjures up an image of frighteningly difficult grammar rules, and the human brain just shuts off. If you approached the test with this idea, for instance, your eye would be drawn to choices C and D in question 1. Many students believe that since English grammar is complex, then an answer on a grammar test will be the most complex one. On the Writing TAAS, the opposite is true more often than not. On question 1, the answer is choice A, the present tense, *argue*.

On question 2, the "less is more" principle still works, but it also demonstrates why you should use this technique to eliminate wrong answer choices, rather than to directly pick out the correct answer. Why do you think I say that, Alexis?

> **Strategy**
>
> In general, the fewer words in the answer choice, the better. On most of the grammar questions, the big three tenses—past, present, future—are usually the correct answers. But don't just pick the answer choice with the fewest words. Instead, eliminate the misleading (and often wrong) answer choices—those tenses that add **been**, **have**, and **are**—and go from there.

Alexis: On question 2 the answer is C. If you had simply picked the answer with the fewest words, you would have incorrectly selected choice A. But if you use the less is more principle first to eliminate unlikely answers, you would have eliminated B and D. That leaves A and C, both of which are well-used tenses, present and future. I picked C. Choice C is correct partly because *continues*, choice A, is singular, while the word *people* is plural.

Jorge: Bravissimo! Remember the "less is more" principle, and you will go far. Now regarding question 5, you don't have to even look at the sentence above to answer this question correctly. Question 5 concerns double negatives, and you may remember that in life, two wrongs do not make a right, and in grammar, two negative words together do not

> **Strategy**
>
> Two negative words together do not make a correct sentence. When answering a question concerning double negatives, eliminate all answer choices that have two or more of the following words: **not**, **never**, **hardly**, **scarcely**, and the contraction **n't**. Also eliminate any answer choices that you know contain improper grammar or imaginary words.

make a correct sentence. So, you can cross out all answer choices except A. In fact, before you read the passage, eliminate any answer choices that you know contain imaginary words or improper grammar, such as choice D on question 3, *importantest*.

In the passage about history on page 87, the first sentence is worthless from a test-taking viewpoint. There's no blank to fill in. Since your primary goal is to answer questions correctly, you don't accomplish that by reading a sentence that has no question in it. Feel free to skip that sentence.

> **Strategy**
>
> *Within the boxed-in passage, read only those sentences that have words missing. Even though it might look interesting, there is no reason to waste time reading the entire passage. Your task is to identify grammar problems, so focus on those.*

Ridley: Jorge, these techniques work well for this section, and they help out on questions 1, 2, and 5, but how we do solve those other questions?

Jorge: You all know some grammar, so you won't need to rely on special techniques for every problem. On any question that you're not sure about, like question 3, sound out the sentence and pick the answer that sounds right.

On question 3, when we sound out the remaining three answer choices, C can be eliminated, since the phrase "learning history is the more importantly thing" is incorrect. That leaves A or B. At this point, trust your ears to lead you to B, the correct answer.

Using the ear technique for questions 4 and 6, the answers are D and C, respectively. This technique works on all grammar questions, and while you are better off actually knowing the proper grammar rules, this will help when you're in doubt.

> **Strategy**
>
> *When you aren't sure of an answer, sound out the sentence to yourself and choose the answer that sounds right. Trust your ears!*

The Middle Third: Spelling, Capitalization and Punctuation (Questions 13–26)

Jorge: The middle third of Writing: Part 1 includes approximately three passages, followed by 14 questions total.

Jonas went to the toolshed and picked out his best hammer. He had a

big repair job <u>on Madison avenue, and he did not</u> want anything to

(13)

go wrong with it. Silently, he went over a mental checklist in his head,

making sure he had <u>the screwdrivers pliers and screws that he needed</u>.

(14)

No one was there at the house when he arrived. He tried knocking on

the <u>front windows, and he rang the doorbell several times, but</u> no one

(15)

answered. Just as Jonas was about to leave, a voice behind him asked

<u>casualy "Are you looking for me?"</u> The man who spoke to Jonas was

(16)

Elvis Presley!!

---

13. A. Spelling error
     B. Capitalization error
     C. Punctuation error
     D. No error

14. A. Spelling error
     B. Capitalization error
     C. Punctuation error
     D. No error

15. A. Spelling error
     B. Capitalization error
     C. Punctuation error
     D. No error

16. A. Spelling error
     B. Capitalization error
     C. Punctuation error
     D. No error

Jorge: As you can see, all questions have the same answer choices. This is typical of what you'll see on the TAAS, although I made up the last sentence about Elvis to see if anyone read it!

To find the right answer, start with choice A, and check for a spelling error. If you don't find one, look for a capitalization error. If you don't find one, look for a punctuation error. If you don't find one, pick choice D.

> O Blue Hawaiian One, do you think we should finally let Elvis go? I know you like his songs, but he keeps escaping, and I think some people are getting suspicious.

X!Frumious: Why should we start with A, and then use POE to move down?

Jorge: Because spelling errors should be the easiest to spot. You just look at the word, and you will know right away if there is a mistake. Capitalization is a little harder, since you have to make some distinction about how the word is used in the sentence. For example, "I asked my father if I could go to the store," is not the same as "I asked Father McSwirly if I could go to the store." In the second sentence, the word *father* is used as a proper noun. Since a proper noun refers to a specific person, place, or thing, it's capitalized. So in the second sentence, "I asked Father McSwirly if I could go to the store" (a specific person), both words are capitalized.

Willy: OK, I'll try this on the previous passage. First, I skip the first sentence, as there's no point in reading it. Then, I look at the underlined portion (13), and look for spelling errors. I don't see any, so now I look for capitalization errors. The word *avenue* should be capitalized, since Madison Avenue is a specific place.

Strategy

Keep your distance from the story-line of the passage, and you'll have an easier time concentrating on finding the right answer. Unless you absolutely must, read only those sentences that contain questions. The more involved you get in the flow of the passage, the more likely you'll overlook something.

Jorge: Great. Then the answer for question 13 is B. And you see, you didn't even have to check for a punctuation error, which is a harder thing to do. Punctuation errors—and on the TAAS, about half of them involve missing commas—are the hardest to spot, since you have to concentrate on the structure of the sentence. Following the same process on the next phrase (14), I looked for spelling and capitalization errors, but didn't find any. However, there is a list of items that needs to be separated by commas, so I picked C for question 14. Question 16 is fairly simple, if you spot the word *casualy* misspelled. Now, Alexis, what about question 15?

Information

2–3 out of 14 questions normally have "No error" as the correct answer choice. In other words, a few questions will be correct as written. Don't sweat it if you can't find the mistake each time.

Strategy

To find the right answer, start at the top—with choice A—and check for a spelling error. If you don't find one, move to choice B and look for a capitalization error. If you don't find one, look for choice C, a punctuation error. If you don't find one, pick choice D.

Alexis: I looked for all three types of errors, and couldn't find one. Now I've crossed out every answer choice except D.

Jorge: Then D must be correct. Recheck your work once, and then have no qualms about picking D, "No error."

The Final Third: Sentence Construction (Questions 27–40)

Jorge: This section also has boxed-in passages followed by questions. In this case, there are four passages per test, with 14 questions total.

Jonas went to the toolshed and picked out his best hammer. <u>He had a big</u>

<u>*repair job on Madison Avenue, and he did not want anything to go*</u>
(27)

<u>*wrong with this big repair job*</u>*. Silently, he went over a mental check list in*

his head <u>making sure he had the screwdrivers, pliers, and screws that</u>
(28)

<u>*he needed.*</u>

No one was there at the house when he arrived. <u>He tried knocking on the</u>

<u>*front windows, he rang the doorbell several times no one answered*</u>*. Just as*
(29)

Jonas was about to leave, a voice behind him asked casually, "Are you

looking for me?" The man who spoke to Jonas was Elvis Presley!!

---

27. A. He had a big repair job on Madison Avenue, but he did not want anything to go wrong with it.
    B. He had a big repair job on Madison Avenue. He did not want anything to go wrong with this big repair job.
    C. Having a big repair job on Madison Avenue, he did not want anything to go wrong with this big repair job.
    D. He had a big repair job on Madison Avenue, and he did not want anything to go wrong with it.

28. A. his head. He was making sure he had the screwdrivers, pliers, and screws that he needed.
    B. his head, making sure he had the screwdrivers pliers and screws that he needed.
    C. of the screwdrivers, pliers, and screws that he needed, making sure they were in his head.
    D. Correct as is

29. A. He tried knocking on the front windows, and he rang the doorbell several times, but no one answered.
    B. He tried knocking on the front windows, he was ringing the doorbell several times, but no one answered
    C. He tried knocking on the front windows, and he rang the doorbell several times, and no one answered.
    D. Correct as is

Jorge: Once again, I recommend not reading any sentence that doesn't have a question attached to it. This section has more of them than the previous two sections, so if you thought it was a waste of time before, just wait until you read an eight-sentence passage only to answer four questions.

On the final third of the Writing TAAS, you do not need to worry about spelling: Everything is spelled correctly. The focus of this section is sentence construction; that is, is the underlined text the best way to state something? Before you ask yourself that question, however, look to see if there is an answer choice that says, "Correct as is." If it is not present, that means the question must have a flaw in it.

X!Frumious: Question 27 has four answers that are all different from the text.

Jorge: We know, then, that the underlined part of question 27 is wrong, and we need to figure out how.

Another indication that the original underlined phrase is incorrect is the presence of the repeated phrase *big repair job*.

The TEA has even provided us with some clues for the final third of this section. At the beginning of the section, the TEA tells you to look for "correctly written sentences that need to be combined," as well as "run-on sentences." Question 27 is a good example of a grammatically correct sentence that needs to be combined, and question 29 is an example of a run-on sentence.

This doesn't mean the sentence is grammatically wrong. If there is a repeated phrase, the sentence could probably be rewritten to be structurally better. In other words, it is a problem with sentence construction, which is the main theme of these questions. After looking to see whether there is a "Correct as is" answer choice, the next step is to go back to the original passage. Focus your thoughts on two things: 1. Replace repeated phrases with the proper pronouns. 2. Make sure the transitional

---

Strategy

When considering whether the underlined portion of the text is the best way to state something, first look to see if there is an answer choice that says, "Correct as is." If it is NOT present, that means the question must have a flaw in it. Then, go back to the original passage and focus on two things:

1. Replace repeated phrases with the appropriate pronouns;

2. Make sure the transitional elements of a sentence— conjunctions like **and**, **or** and **but** as well as **commas**—are being used correctly.

elements of a sentence—conjunctions like *and, or* and *but* as well as commas—are being used correctly.

These are the two favorite construction errors in this section. For instance, in question 27, you need to eliminate the second *big repair job* and replace it with the pronoun *it*. This leaves you with A and D. Now check the transitional elements. Which is better for the sentence, *and* or *but*?

> **Information**
>
> *Repeated phrases within an underlined section almost always mean that the sentence needs to be rewritten.*

Alexis: I say it's D, since the two sentences are connected to each other, and not opposed.

Jorge: Right. On question 28, look at the question to see if the original phrase could be the proper sentence construction. Answer D, "Correct as is," is there. Now, looking at the original phrase, see if you can find any repeated phrases or if you think the transitional elements are messed up in some way. If nothing seems wrong, then pick D, and move on. About 2–4 questions in this section will be "Correct as is." Moving on to question 29, you should be able to notice that it is a run-on sentence.

Ridley: I did notice, Jorge, and so I starting checking the answer choices. Choice A looked correct to me, so do I need to look any further?

Jorge: Yes, you should, because even though choice A looks good, there might be an answer choice that looks even better. Say that you cross out B and D, but C doesn't appear to be that bad of an answer. I would choose between A and C, and pick A, since it is the best way to rewrite that run-on sentence.

Overview: Writing TAAS Part 1 Strategies

Strategy 1: *On grammar questions, the big three tenses—past, present, future—are usually the correct answers. In general, the fewer words in the answer choice, the better.*

Strategy 2: *Within boxed-in reading passages, read only those sentences that have questions or contain blanks. Even if the passage looks like interesting reading, don't waste time reading it all. Instead, focus on the sentences with grammar problems.*

Strategy 3: *Before you read a passage, eliminate any answer choices that you know contain improper grammar or imaginary words.*

Strategy 4: *When you aren't sure of an answer, sound out the sentence to yourself and choose the answer choice that sounds right. Trust your ears!*

Strategy 5: *Keep your distance from the storyline of the passage. That way, you'll have an easier time concentrating on finding the right answer. The more involved you get in the flow of the passage, the more likely you'll overlook something.*

Strategy 6: *On **Spelling**, **Capitalization**, and **Punctuation** questions, work down to find the flaw in the phrase—start with choice A and check the phrase for a spelling error. If there isn't one, move on to choice B, and look for a capitalization error. Moving down through the answer choices, use elimination to help you narrow in on the problem.*

Strategy 7: *To help you correct flaws in **Sentence Construction** questions, a) replace any repeated phrases with appropriate pronouns; and b) make sure the transitional elements of the sentence—conjunctions like **and**, **or**, and **but**, as well as **commas**—are being used correctly. Remember, this doesn't always mean the sentence is grammatically wrong, it just means that there's probably a better way to state it.*

Sample Questions–Writing

Three friends of mine from biology class have recently started playing in a jazz

band called The Pallid Armadillos. _____ play at weddings, festivals, and

(1)

sometimes even restaurants. After they pay for the cost of renting stereo

equipment, the three friends _____ the money equally between them after

(2)

each show. To show their support, some of the parents helped the band make

some music contacts in the city. This enabled The Pallid Armadillos to get off to a

_____ start.

(3)

Jeremy, the singer, _____ in music since he was very young. His best friend,

(4)

Laura, _____ really into playing in a band at first, but then Jeremy

(5)

convinced her. Now, Laura is _____ the best performer in the group,

(6)

constantly talking to the audience and getting them into the act.

---

1. A. She
    B. He
    C. It
    D. They

2. A. split
    B. are splitting
    C. were splitting
    D. will split

3. A. well
    B. good
    C. better
    D. best

4. A. has been interested
    B. was interested
    C. interests
    D. is interested

5. A. was not never
    B. isn't hardly
    C. wasn't
    D. was not scarcely

6. A. easiest
    B. more easily
    C. most easiest
    D. easily

Jonathan was nervous about his first job interview. His mother had helped prepare him for the kind of questions _that were usualy asked, but Jonathan still_ was not

(7)

sure he was ready. _What if the interviewer asked him a really tough question_.

(8)

Jonathan was normally a fairly confident person, but this experience was something he had never done before.

A _secretary came up and told Jonathan that Mr. Frick, the store manager,_ was ready

(9)

to see him now. Randall Frick was a thin, smiling man who had been the _manager of osgood's supermarket for over twenty years._ "Come in and have a seat,

(10)

son," he said _warmly. "is this your first job interview?" he asked._

(11)

The first question was one Jonathan could easily _answer. "Yes, ser, it is."_ Once he

(12)

started talking, Jonathan lost most of the nervousness he had. He and Mr. Frick talked for _about thirty minutes about various topics, like_

(13)

sports school and history. When the interview was over, Jonathan had a job.

7. A. Spelling error
    B. Capitalization error
    C. Punctuation error
    D. No error

8. A. Spelling error
    B. Capitalization error
    C. Punctuation error
    D. No error

9. A. Spelling error
    B. Capitalization error
    C. Punctuation error
    D. No error

10. A. Spelling error
    B. Capitalization error
    C. Punctuation error
    D. No error

11. A. Spelling error
    B. Capitalization error
    C. Punctuation error
    D. No error

12. A. Spelling error
    B. Capitalization error
    C. Punctuation error
    D. No error

13. A. Spelling error
    B. Capitalization error
    C. Punctuation error
    D. No error

You might think it would be fun to play video games all day, but don't be so sure.

Just ask <u>Rand Diaz about it he spent an entire summer working as a tester for a video</u>
(14)

<u>game company.</u> In fact, Rand still works as a video game tester. <u>While the job</u>

<u>sounds very easy, the job is actually hard work.</u> Playing video games requires
(15)

concentration and constant use of your reflexes. Concentrating for eight hours

every day can be pretty <u>tiring. This is because it takes a great deal of mental effort.</u>
(16)

Rand said that when he first started, he used to get headaches. However,

<u>once he began to stand farther away from the video screen,</u> the headaches stopped.
(17)

---

14. A. Rand Diaz about it, he spent an entire summer working, as a tester for a video game company.
    B. Rand Diaz about it, he spent an entire summer working as a tester for a video game company.
    C. Rand Diaz about it. He spent an entire summer working as a tester for a video game company.
    D. Correct as is

15. A. While the job sounds very easy, it is actually hard work.
    B. While the job sounds very easy. It is actually hard work.
    C. While the job sounds very easy. The job is actually hard work.
    D. The job, while it sounds very easy it is actually hard work.

16. A. every day can be pretty tiring this is because it takes a great deal of mental effort.
    B. every day can be pretty tiring because it takes a great deal of mental effort.
    C. every day can be pretty tiring, this is because it takes a great deal of mental effort.
    D. Correct as is

17. A. However. Once, he began to stand farther away from the video screen,
    B. However once he began to stand farther away from the video screen
    C. However; once, he began to stand farther away from the video screen,
    D. Correct as is

Whenever people hear the word fossil, *they <u>usually think of one thing: dinosaur</u>*
<u>bones.</u> However, there are many different kinds of fossils besides dinosaur bones.
For example, scientists find many <u>come from animals, and these animals, they</u>
<u>existed long before the dinosaurs</u> ever walked the earth. Many of these fossils are
found in the sea, since objects that come to rest on the ocean floor often <u>do not</u>
<u>decompose at all, instead, they lie</u> on the ocean floor and are gradually covered
by sediment, which covers the skeleton of the dead animal and slowly turns the
animal into a fossil.

18. A. usually think of one thing,
       "dinosaur bones."
   B. usually think of one thing;
       Dinosaur bones.
   C. usually think of one thing.
       Dinosaur bones.
   D. Correct as is

20. A. do not decompose, at all,
       instead they lie
   B. do not decompose. At all
       instead, they lie
   C. do not decompose at all.
       Instead, they lie
   D. Correct as is

19. A. fossils that come from
       animals, these animals
       existing long before the
       dinosaurs
   B. fossils that come from
       animals that existed long
       before the dinosaurs
   C. fossils that come from
       animals, and these animals,
       they and their fossils existed
       long before the dinosaurs
   D. fossils coming from animals
       and they existed long before
       the dinosaurs

Writing TAAS Part 2

Session Leader: Willy H_2SO_4

> O Your Pookiness, our fifth meeting was going to be held in Willy's garage, but it seems Willy's parents have asked him to never set foot in the garage again. We held the meeting in Willy's old treehouse instead, which was quite cozy!
> —X!Frumious

NAME: William Bruce Walker, better known as Willy H_2SO_4

BORN: February 17, 1984
Fort Worth, Texas

NOTES: A chemistry buff, Willy once made soap from materials he collected on a Boy Scout nature trip into Big Bend State Park. He then wrote the essay, "How Cleaning Your Hands in the Middle of a Desert is a Character-Building Experience," which earned him the Best Essay of the Year from his grade school. A garage accident also earned Willy his nickname, although sulfuric acid was not actually used. He owns one pet, a coati mundi name Heisenberg.

Jorge: (looking around the treehouse) William, this treehouse is amazingly decorated. I love the stuffed moose you have in the corner.

Willy: Yes, it wasn't easy to get him up the tree, but it was well worth it. I want to bring up a small piano next, but my parents aren't very keen about the idea. Enough talk of music. Let's get down to business, shall we?

The Essay

On Writing TAAS Part 2, you will be required to write an essay (also called a written composition). The essay is graded on a scale of 1 to 4. The minimum passing score is 2. A score of 0 means that the essay was incomprehensible, or way off topic, such as when you have written a letter to the Mayor of Houston demanding that students be allowed to have special parking permits when you were asked to write about the pros and cons of traffic rules.

While the rest of the exam is scored by computer, your essay will be read by two teachers who will each decide on a score from 1–4. If they agree, that's your score for the essay section. If they disagree— say one reader wants to give your essay a 2, but the other thinks it deserves a 3—then your essay is given to a third reader, who acts as a tiebreaker. While the process is a little arbitrary, the readers are experienced at doing this, so you don't need to worry about your essay suffering simply because a reader slammed his foot in his car door that morning.

Overview: Writing TAAS

Format

Part 1	40 multiple-choice questions on grammar, spelling, capitalization and punctuation
Part 2	written essay (composition)

Scoring

Part 1: *Multiple-Choice Questions*	If your essay score is 4, 7 out of 40 questions must be answered correctly. If your essay score is 3, 17 out of 40 questions must be answered correctly. If your essay score is 2, 27 out of 40 questions must be answered correctly.
Part 2: *Essay*	Graded scale from 1 to 4; 2 is the minimum passing score.
Time given for test	untimed

Overview: Writing TAAS (Essay) Objectives

TAAS Objective	What it Means
1. The student will respond appropriately to the purpose/audience specified in a given topic.	Write your essay on the topic you are asked to write on.
2. The student will organize ideas on a given topic.	Make sure your essay has the proper structure, such as sentences, paragraphs, and related thoughts organized together.
3. The student will demonstrate control of the English language.	Don't use the word **cat** when you mean **dog**. Also, keep the number of grammar and spelling errors to a minimum.
4. The student will generate a written composition that develops/supports/elaborates the central idea stated in a given topic.	Whatever your main idea is, you'd better provide some information to back up your statement.

Jorge: What objectives does this section deal with?

Willy: TAAS Objectives 1–4: Writing Skills. In fact, these are the criteria that readers use to grade your essay. Now, you might think, "the essay is worth four points, and there are four objectives. That means I get a point for each objective. Right?"

X!Frumious: Sounds good to me.

Willy: Sounds good, but it's wrong. While all four objectives are important, the information you provide to support your main idea (Objective 4) is the most important factor in your essay score.

Of course, if you don't have the first three objectives down pat, the amount of supporting information you provide is irrelevant. In other words, if you don't meet Objective 1, and you write about a completely different topic than the one you're supposed to write about, you're heading for a score of 0. And if don't organize your thoughts (Objective 2), but instead just write them down as soon as you think of them—that's an essay hovering between 0 and 1. You'll be heading for a similar score if you don't use English in a comprehensible manner (Objective 3).

> **Strategy**
>
> While you should strive to meet all of the writing objectives, the most important factor in your essay score will be how well you use information to support your main idea (Objective 4).

Jorge: I understand the first two points you made, but how do you define "English in a comprehensible manner?" I am fortunate to be a foreigner who speaks English well, but I know that I'm an exception, rather than the rule.

Willy: That's true, Jorge, but the key is to write English well enough to be understood. If you write the sentence "People should not to be out after curfew hours," it won't matter that you have improper verb phrasing in the predicate because the sentence is still comprehensible. The key is to justify why "people should not to be out after curfew." There would, however, be a problem if the above statement looked like "people are out after curfew." In this sentence fragment, there is no point being made, and this essay would suffer.

Improper grammar may prevent you from getting a 4 on the essay, but it won't stop you from getting a 2, which is what you need to pass.

Imperfect grammar won't kill your essay, but poor supporting details will. To illustrate how focused the

> **Strategy**
>
> As long as your English is understandable, inexact grammar won't cripple your essay. Poor supporting details, however, will cripple your essay. Strive for an essay that provides thorough, clear, and convincing support for your main idea.

TEA is on proper use of supporting details in the essay, take a look at the chart below. It shows the four levels of detail, or elaboration, that the TEA uses when evaluating each essay.

Overview: Writing TAAS Scoring Chart

Levels of Detail, or Elaboration, Used for Essay Evaluation

TEA Name	Description
Extended response	Writer links main idea to one additional piece of information.
Somewhat elaborated	Writer provides another piece of information that further clarifies a reader's understanding of the essay.
Moderately elaborated	Writer clarifies the main idea in even greater detail.
Fully elaborated	Writer develops a reason that provides a thorough, clearly understood, and convincing support for the main idea.

There are four levels, and the essay is graded from 1–4. Another coincidence? Maybe, maybe not. Suffice it to say, the level of supporting detail you provide in your essay is a major factor of your score.

The Writing Prompt

Willy: Now that you have some idea about the grading and structure behind the essay, let's talk about the essay itself. On Part 2 of the Writing TAAS, you will see a prompt—a statement of some sort followed by the question, "What is your position regarding this issue?" Here's a sample.

Recently a school board was given control of a large plot of land directly behind the school's baseball field. Some members of the Student Council are recommending to the school board that the land should be made into a park.

What is your position concerning this issue? Write a letter to the president of your school board stating your position and supporting it with convincing reasons. Be sure to explain your reasons in detail.

Your first consideration is, do you support the park plan or not? It doesn't matter what side of the argument you take. All that matters is how well you support your argument.

Information

As the writing prompt indicates, the emphasis is on how well you support your main idea, not what side of the argument you take.

Ridley: So "I like the park idea" is not the correct answer?

Willy: Right, and "I do not like the park idea" isn't correct, either. There are no correct answers, only well-supported arguments versus poorly supported arguments. So once you have decided which side of the argument you want to support, start planning your essay.

Notice I didn't say, "start writing your essay." The key to any good essay is good planning, so there's no need to start writing frantically. Remember, the key is to pass the TAAS, not set a new land-speed record by finishing it in five minutes. The Writing TAAS is untimed, as is every TAAS test, and you should take at least 5–10 minutes to plan your essay. Take the time to plan out your reasons in the best detail as possible.

I suggest writing out numbers for each of your supporting ideas, and then developing each one into fuller detail and explanation. For instance, let's say my main statement is, "I like fresh fruit better than rotten fruit." I should now come up with several connected reasons that explain why I like fresh fruit.

Strategy

After you read the prompt, decide which side of the argument you want to support, and then start planning your essay.

Ridley: You want to come up with a minimum of four reasons because the TEA has four different stages of elaboration, right?

Willy: Exactly. If I only said, "I like fresh fruit because it tastes good," then I would get only an extended response, and I'm shooting for fully elaborated. Therefore, in my planning stage I would write on a scratch sheet of paper:

Main idea: I like fresh fruit better than rotten fruit.

1.   *Fresh fruit tastes better than rotten fruit, so I'll probably enjoy fresh fruit more.*

2.   *Since I enjoy eating fresh fruit, I eat a lot of it, and since fruit is nutritious, I improve my health by doing so.*

3.   *Rotten fruit could have diseases or bacteria that will make me sick after eating it, while with fresh fruit that probably won't happen.*

4.   *Fresh fruit is easier to find in stores, as most of them don't sell rotten fruit (although I could buy fresh fruit on my own and then let it rot, but it would take a while.)*

5.   *Some types of rotting fruit eventually become foods of their own (such as grapes changing into raisins), but if I wanted to eat raisins I'd buy a box of raisins, and if I wanted to eat grapes, I'd buy fresh grapes.*

Information

Do NOT plan your essay on the two lined pages provided in the test booklet, since that space is needed for the essay and nothing else. Use the blank space on the writing prompt page to jot down notes instead.

Keep in mind this is the planning stage, so some of my reasons will be better than others. I was just brainstorming ideas. Looking over them, reason 1 is good, and the fact that reason 2 links into it makes those two good additional information. Reason 3 is pretty good, but if I could find a way to expound that idea some more, I would help myself out. Reasons 4 and 5 are helpful because they show I'm trying to look at both sides of the argument. In reason 5, I take the pro–rotten fruit side and claim that some rotting foods become food of their own, but then I quickly refute that and reinforce my original idea.

Ridley: You wrote out five reasons for the fruit argument. Do we need only five reasons?

Willy: No. The more reasons you can come with, the better, so long as they help prove your point. Also, the more reasons you have that link together—such as 1 and 2 above—the better off you are. The planning stage is where you make or break your essay, so take the time to think about the writing prompt and come up with as many compelling reasons as you can. If you come up with 20 reasons, then take the time to decide which of those are the best ones, and figure out how those reasons best fit together. Also, make sure you know your audience. What you would write to one group of people would not necessarily be the same as what you would write to another group of people. Then, compose your essay.

To guide you through a mock essay, let's take the original writing prompt about the proposed park. My first question is, "Do I want to support the park idea or not?" In this case, I'm not going to support the Student Council position. Instead, I'm going to offer my own proposal for how to use the land. I believe an organic vegetable garden would be a better idea for the land. Now that I've decided what position I will choose, it's time to brainstorm reasons. Here are some of my notes.

Ideas for Organic Vegetable Farm Essay

1. *Offers a variety of unique learning opportunities in both farming and science.*

2. *Gives students a good reason to be outside on a beautiful day.*

3. *Sale of vegetables could be used to fund field trips and other activities.*

4. *Hands-on experience in farming could give students a helpful advantage in summer internships.*

5. *Vegetable sale can be run as a business, giving people work experience.*

6. *Students on detention can pick weeds.*

7. *No other school has an organic vegetable farm, making us stand out.*

8. *New school mascot: Binky, the additive-free rutabaga.*

Willy: Having brainstormed this group of ideas, the next step is to decide on the best sequence to put them in. Organize your ideas in a clear, logical way.

Remember, the readers at TEA want to see fully elaborated reasons, so I won't just write these eight thoughts down in the order I thought of them. Looking them over, I think I can group some of the related points. For instance, I think Ideas 1, 4, and 5 are closely connected, since they all related to using the farm for learning purposes. I could write a paragraph in my essay that looks something like this.

Dear School Board President,

Instead of using the vacant space next to the school for a park, I would like to suggest an alternate use. There are currently numerous parks throughout the city, and while everyone enjoys green spaces, I believe we could do better here at Eastbury High. That's right: I'm thinking what you're thinking—let's start an organic vegetable farm.

Having an organic vegetable farm would provide a wealth of learning opportunities for our students. Students in botany could get hands-on experience dealing with plants and how they grow, something that I believe most other high school students do not get in their school. Science students could also use the garden to learn more about genetics, as they could combine plants with different traits to see what occurs. Any vegetables grown in the garden could then be eaten by students or— better yet—sold in order to raise funds for various school activities, like field trips and school dances. If you put students in charge of selling the produce, then these students would gain valuable business experience, learning all about the sale and pricing of fruits and vegetables.

Information

An effective essay is one in which information is organized in a clear, logical way. After you have brain-stormed for ideas, think about how to order, develop, and connect each one. Think about the audience for whom you are writing and about what language would be most appropriate.

Willy: I could go on with this paragraph, but I think you get the point. On the real essay I would definitely continue, because the more related points I can string together, the closer my chances are that I reach full elaboration.

Daniel: Sounds good so far, but what about the other ideas? I don't see how you are going to attach the mascot idea to anything.

Willy: Then I won't use it. I don't have to use all of the ideas I first thought of, and if I come up with anything while writing, I can always include those.

One other paragraph I should include in my essay is the one where I look at the possible objections to having an organic garden, and then reject them one by one. This shows I understand both sides of the argument.

I know that there are many close-minded people out there who have always been against the marriage of schools and organic farms. They might claim that learning about farming is pointless, since most high school students will never farm again in their lives, and even people who do become real farmers will do so on massive farms which use computerized harvesters and automated sprinklers. Anyone who claims that learning about farming is pointless is missing the entire point of education, which is to learn things and become a better person. Maybe none of us will become farmers. So what? That shouldn't stop us from having a garden of our own when we are older and growing our own vegetables, which are almost always superior to grocery store produce in both size and quality.

> **Strategy**
>
> Always try to present an understanding of both sides of the argument. If you can describe the other side's position, and reasons why you disagree with it, then you have helped your own argument and boosted your essay.

Other critics might claim that the idea is "crazy" just because no one has done it before. To this I ask, what better way to instill a spirit of pride in a school that to do something no one has done before? School morale is important to a school—if we had an organic garden, that would set us apart from all the other schools, and school spirit would become very visible. Having a mascot like "The Farmer" is not very threatening, but at least it's accurate. I happen to know for a fact that our current mascot, the tiger, has never roamed the lands around Houston.

Willy: Again, I could go on, but I think you get the point.

Finally, before you start writing out your essay, there is one last thing you need to bear in mind: write neatly. Readers cannot and will not grade what they cannot read.

If you have poor cursive penmanship, make sure you print out your essay. Make it as easy as you can for the readers to read your handwriting, or your essay score will suffer.

> **Strategy**
>
> Make sure you write neatly. Readers cannot and will not grade what they cannot read.

Overview: Three-Step Method for TAAS Essay Writing

Step 1: Think

- First, plan your essay. Brainstorm ideas, writing down whatever comes to your mind in support of your point. Use numbers to list your points, elaborating on every idea.

- Select your best ideas and decide how to clearly connect them together. Your goal is to persuade your audience of your point of view. Your essay must flow, so use transition words and ideas to link your ideas.

- Use language and tone that are appropriate for your audience.

- Take a strong stand **for** or **against** the idea expressed in the prompt.

Step 2: Write

- Your essay should be 3–4 paragraphs in length. It should contain an introduction, a body, and a conclusion.

- Introduction: States your argument and briefly describes the reasons you will provide in support of that argument.

- Body paragraph(s): Explains the reasons behind your argument. Support your reasons with facts and examples. If you decide on one long body paragraph, make sure that it's clear to the reader where one reason ends and the next begins.

- Conclusion: Briefly restates your argument and the reasons behind it, using somewhat different language.

Step 3: Repair

- Your first draft is not your final draft. Once you've finished writing your essay, revise and proofread it.

- Neatness counts!—make certain that your handwriting is legible.

Chapter 6

Epilogue

TO: X!Frumious the Explorer, currently stationed on Earth

FROM: The Most Supreme Ruler of the planet Kronhorst

RE: Your notes about the Exit-Level TAAS

Dear X!Frumious,

Having read your notes about the Exit TAAS, I can easily remember why you are my favorite Kronhorstian out of all my loyal subjects. Thorough work! I learned quite a bit about standardized tests, and I am quite eager to try some of those tasty charcoal briquettes you were eating earlier.

Your study group notes convinced me to learn more about the TAAS on my own, so I used my human Internet connection and checked out the Texas Education Agency web site at **www.tea.state.tx.us**. It contained a wealth of information concerning not only the TAAS, but various other educational issues occurring in Texas. I also thought it would be fun to try taking some old, released versions of the Exit-Level TAAS, so I called 1-800-252-9186 and ordered some past exams. They cost only $1 each. I am sure that many human schools have already purchased these materials for their students, but it's nice to know that even if you are an alien from a distant galaxy, you can still get hold of some TAAS tests, so long as you're willing to fork over the cash.

I am very eager to learn how well you do on the Exit-Level TAAS when you take it. However, regardless of how well you do, I want you to remember that this test is only one part of your educational career. Granted, it is an important milestone, and all human students need to pass it to graduate high school, but getting a poor score on the TAAS does not mean you are a bad student. It might mean you had a bad day, or that you are a poor standardized test taker, or that you need to brush on some basic skills before you take the test again. While the tests provide an interesting snapshot of your educational career, they capture only one moment of your education, and don't shed light on the full length motion picture movie that is your entire academic career. So, if you do fail one or more of the TAAS tests, the people I will talk to first will be the people who know your academic standing better than anyone else—your teachers there at Eastbury High. They will be able to look over your scores and tell me how they relate to you as a student. Until I hear from them, I will not interpret your TAAS scores as anything more than how well you did on one set of standardized tests.

That's all for now. Come back to Kronhorst soon—Mrs. Supreme Ruler of the planet Kronhorst misses you, as do I. If you ever need any help tutoring, drop by the palace and we'll work on some test questions together.

Stay relaxed and do the best you can on the Exit-Level TAAS. That's all anyone can ask from you, including me. Well, gotta go—there's a planet to run, you know. I remain

       Your Loving Father,

       X!Frumious, Sr.

       X!Frumious, Sr.
       Supreme Ruler of Kronhorst, Most Scaly One, etc.

P. S. Why don't you bring your study group over for dinner sometime?

Answer Key: Sample Questions

Mathematics

Concepts (TAAS Questions 1–20)			Problem Solving (TAAS Questions 21–44)			Operations (TAAS Questions 45–60)		
	Answer	Objective Tested		Answer	Objective Tested		Answer	Objective Tested
1.	C	4	11.	D	12	23.	E	6
2.	C	5	12.	E	13	24.	A	7
3.	B	1	13.	C	10	25.	E	9
4.	D	5	14.	A	11	26.	B	8
5.	B	3	15.	B	12	27.	C	9
6.	D	2	16.	E	12	28.	E	6
7.	A	2	17.	E	12	29.	A	7
8.	C	4	18.	B	13	30.	B	8
9.	A	1	19.	C	11			
10.	B	3	20.	C	11			
			21.	D	10			
			22.	A	11			

Reading

	Answer	Objective Tested		Answer	Objective Tested
1.	D	6	11.	B	5
2.	C	4	12.	C	6
3.	A	5	13.	A	5
4.	C	3	14.	D	4
5.	B	5	15.	C	3
6.	D	5	16.	A	5
7.	B	2	17.	C	2
8.	D	1	18.	B	4
9.	B	3	19.	A	5
10.	A	1	20.	D	6

Writing

	Answer	Objective Tested		Answer	Objective Tested
1.	D	6	11.	B	7
2.	A	6	12.	A	7
3.	B	6	13.	C	7
4.	A	6	14.	C	5
5.	C	6	15.	A	5
6.	D	6	16.	B	5
7.	A	7	17.	D	5
8.	C	7	18.	D	5
9.	D	7	19.	B	5
10.	B	7	20.	C	5

How Did We Do? Grade Us.

Thank you for choosing a Kaplan book. Your comments and suggestions are very useful to us. Please answer the following questions to assist us in our continued development of high-quality resources to meet your needs.

e Kaplan book I read was: _____

name is: _____

address is: _____

_____

e-mail address is: _____

at overall grade would you give this book? (A) (B) (C) (D) (F)

w relevant was the information to your goals? (A) (B) (C) (D) (F)

w comprehensive was the information in this book? (A) (B) (C) (D) (F)

w accurate was the information in this book? (A) (B) (C) (D) (F)

w easy was the book to use? (A) (B) (C) (D) (F)

w appealing was the book's design? (A) (B) (C) (D) (F)

at were the book's strong points? _____

w could this book be improved? _____

here anything that we left out that you wanted to know more about?

uld you recommend this book to others? ☐ YES   ☐ NO

er comments: _____

_____

_____

we have permission to quote you? ☐ YES   ☐ NO

nk you for your help. Please tear out this page and mail it to:

Dave Chipps, Managing Editor
Kaplan Educational Centers
888 Seventh Avenue
New York, NY 10106

ou can answer these questions online at www.kaplan.com/talkback.

ıks!

SIXTY · YEARS · OF
KAPLAN
60
BUILDING · FUTURES

About

KAPLAN®

Educational Centers

Kaplan Educational Centers is one of the nation's leading providers of education and career services. Kaplan is a wholly owned subsidiary of The Washington Post Company.

TEST PREPARATION & ADMISSIONS

Kaplan's nationally recognized test prep courses cover more than 20 standardized tests, including secondary school, college and graduate school entrance exams and foreign language and professional licensing exams. In addition, Kaplan offers private tutoring and comprehensive, one-to-one admissions and application advice for students applying to college and graduate programs. Kaplan also provides information and guidance on the financial aid process. Students can enroll in online test prep courses and admissions consulting services at www.kaptest.com

SCORE! EDUCATIONAL CENTERS

SCORE! after-school learning centers help K-9 students build confidence, academic and goal-setting skills in a motivating, sports-oriented environment. Its cutting-edge, interactive curriculum continually assesses and adapts to each child's academic needs and learning style. Enthusiastic Academic Coaches serve as positive role models, creating a high-energy atmosphere where learning is exciting and fun. SCORE! Prep provides in-home, one-on-one tutoring for high school academic subjects and standardized tests. www.eSCORE.com provides customized online educational resources and services for parents and kids ages 0 to 18. eSCORE.com creates a deep, evolving profile for each child based on his or her age, interests and skills. Parents can access personalized information and resources designed to help their children realize their full potential.

KAPLAN LEARNING SERVICES

Kaplan Learning Services provides customized assessment, education and professional development programs to K-12 schools and universities.

KAPLAN INTERNATIONAL PROGRAMS

Kaplan services international students and professionals in the U.S. through a series of intensive English language and test preparation programs. These programs are offered campus-based centers across the USA. Kaplan offers specialized services including housing, placement at top American universities, fellowship management, academic monitoring and reporting, and financial administration.

KAPLAN PUBLISHING

Kaplan Publishing produces books and software. Kaplan Book joint imprint with Simon & Schuster, publishes titles in test pr ration, admissions, education, career development and life s Kaplan and Newsweek jointly publish guides on getting into coll finding the right career, and helping your child succeed in sc Through an alliance with Knowledge Adventure, Kaplan publis educational software for the K-12 retail and school markets.

KAPLAN PROFESSIONAL

Kaplan Professional provides assessment, training, and cert tion services for corporate clients and individuals seekin advance their careers. Member units include Dearborn, a ing supplier of licensing training and continuing educatio securities, real estate, and insurance professionals; Pe Access/CRN, which delivers software education and consult for law firms and businesses; and Kaplan Professional Call C Services, a total provider of services for the call center indus

DISTANCE LEARNING DIVISION

Kaplan's distance learning programs include Concord Scho Law, the nation's first online law school; and Kaplan Colle leading provider of degree and certificate programs in crimina tice and paralegal studies.

COMMUNITY OUTREACH

Kaplan provides educational career resources to thousands of cially disadvantaged students annually, working closely with e tional institutions, not-for-profit groups, government agencies other grass roots organizations on a variety of national and support programs. Kaplan enriches local communities by emp high school, college and graduate students, creating valuable experiences for vast numbers of young people each year.

BRASSRING

BrassRing Inc., headquartered in New York and San Mateo, the first network that combines recruiting, career developmer hiring management services to serve employers and employe every step. Through its units BrassRing.com and HireSys BrassRing provides an array of on- and off-line resources tha employers simplify and accelerate the hiring process, and individuals to build skills and find a better job. Kapl BrassRing's majority shareholder.

Want more information about our services, products, or the nearest Kaplan center?

1 Call our nationwide toll-free numbers:

1-800-KAP-TEST for information on our courses, private tutoring and admissions consulting

1-800-KAP-ITEM for information on our books and software

1-888-KAP-LOAN* for information on student loans

2 Connect with us in cyberspace:

On AOL, keyword:"Kaplan"
On the World Wide Web, go to:
1. www.kaplan.com
2. www.kaptest.com
3. www.eSCORE.com
4. www.dearborn.com
5. www.BrassRing.com
6. www.concord.kaplan.edu
7. www.kaplancollege.com
Via e-mail: info@kaplan.com

3  Write to:

Kaplan Educational Centers
888 Seventh Avenue
New York, NY 10106

Just in case the rock star thing doesn't work out.

Kaplan gets you in.

For over 60 years, Kaplan has been helping students get into college. Whether you're facing the SAT, PSAT or ACT, take Kaplan and get the score you need to get into the schools you want.

1-800-KAP-TEST
kaptest.com AOL keyword: kaplan

*Test names are registered trademarks of their respective owners.

World Leader in Test Pr